Encyclopaedia of
Great Men of India

Encyclopaedia of Great Men of India

Vol. II
The Great Leaders and Statesmen

Edited by
L. F. Rushbrook Williams

SHUBHI PUBLICATIONS
DELHI

Distributed by
APH Publishing Corp.
5, Ansari Road
Daryaganj, New Delhi

Indian Edition · 1999
ISBN 81-87226-10-2 (set)

Published by
Shubhi Publication
FK-30, Shastri Nagar, Delhi

Printed at :
Efficient Offset

CONTENTS

PANDIT MADAN MOHAN MALAVIYA
The great supporter of Hindu Orthodoxy.

PANDIT MADAN MOHAN MALAVIYA

UPHOLDER OF THE HINDU FAITH

BORN 1862

BY C. F. ANDREWS

I CAN best begin to describe the character of Pandit Madan Mohan Malaviya by a short story of what happened in my own experience long ago; for though outwardly it was of very little consequence, it seemed to open out to me a world of human kindness beneath the forbidding exterior of his scrupulous Hindu orthodoxy, and for this reason it may be worth repeating.

Mr. Gokhale had come back from South Africa, in 1912—ill both in body and mind. In the following year he had been profoundly stirred to action in India itself by the news of the heroic struggle that Mr. Gandhi was carrying on to obtain the barest elementary rights for the distressed Indian labourers suffering under the indenture system. In October, 1913, the passive resistance struggle in South Africa had at last reached its final stage. Indians were brutally treated as they tried to leave the estates, and there was a serious danger of violence breaking out on an extensive scale. Mr. and Mrs. Gandhi, along with their sons, were in prison, and thousands of Indians, both men and women, had gone to prison also. The moral support of India was behind Mr. Gokhale in seeking to prevent the movement from being crushed through any lack of public support. At this time W. W. Pearson had volunteered to accompany me to South Africa in order to take part in the struggle. We had said good-bye to Mr. Gokhale at Delhi, and intended to wait for a few hours at Allahabad in order to see Pundit Madan Mohan Malaviya. We were on our way to Calcutta, where we were to embark for Durban.

Mr. Gokhale had wired to Malaviya to meet the train. He was a personal friend, and we well knew his orthodox Hindu mode of life. He had prepared food for us in his own home; but the train was running very late and we had no time to leave the station. So instead he insisted, in spite of all our protests, in taking us to the refreshment room (where meat was usually served) and sat with us while we took the vegetarian dishes which he had ordered. The European passengers, who were having their breakfast, wondered who this strange Indian was with his immaculately white *pagri* and *chaddar* and his very distinguished features. One or two recognised him. But he used every moment of his time in sending messages through us to the heroic passive resisters in South Africa. His own caste scruples had been laid on one side for our sakes in order to show us this last act of hospitality before we sailed.

It would be difficult to explain the significance of this in England where caste scruples are not understood, but here in India the story, simple as it is, can be easily appreciated. It happened nearly thirty years ago; and things have moved very far forward since those days.

More, perhaps, than any other national leader of the present generation, Pundit Madan Mohan Malaviya has stood out for Hindu orthodoxy in its most binding religious form. This scrupulous exactness of religious observance has made him undergo incredible hardships in the name of his religion which he holds so dear.

In his extreme Hindu outlook lies the main difference between himself and every other leader of first rank in Indian politics to-day. I do not know any outstanding personality who carries his orthodoxy as far as Malaviya. He is conservative to the last degree in everything where Hinduism is concerned, while at the same time in national affairs he is in many respects an advanced thinker. For this reason a conflict is always going on within, between his Hindu orthodoxy and his Indian Nationalism. Divided loyalties tear him asunder; but whenever it comes to a tug of war, Hinduism wins. More and more, as he has grown older, Hindu loyalty has prevailed and Indian Nationalism, as such, has tended to recede into the background.

It may be argued that he has recently stood in the very forefront of the battle for the removal of untouchability, which was one of the standing disgraces of popular Hinduism. But on that subject Panditji had already shared the opinion of Mahatma Gandhi, that such a custom was not Hindu at all. It could not be found—so he asserted—in any of the Hindu Scriptures; furthermore, it was historically unknown in the earliest Sanskrit period. In long arguments I have often heard him argue this point again and again. He would quote passage after passage to show that men of the lowest caste, on account of their purity of character and nobility of life, had been the preceptors of members belonging to the highest castes, teaching them religious truths. How could such men have ever been regarded as polluted and untouchable by those whom they instructed? Thus he would argue; and when the tide of reform swept over the country, and millions of these very people were already wavering in their allegiance towards Hinduism, he anticipated the rapidly impending crisis and pronounced

in favour of the complete abolition of this hateful and inhuman custom, using himself the strongest words about it and causing a great sensation. Indeed, as a Brahman, he went so far as to receive back into Hinduism, by a purifying ceremony, large numbers of those who had left it for other religious faiths.

Yet when, on the other hand, another injurious custom within Hinduism, called "Child Marriage," was brought forward in the Central Assembly for legislative action he objected vehemently to any State legislation on the subject. In this matter he seems to have believed, along with many Pundits of the south, that such child marriages had the sanction of the sacred Hindu scriptures. Any legislation, therefore, was regarded by him as an act of religious persecution, or at least an interference with religion—if the State declared such marriages to be illegal.

Wherein, then, lies the real greatness of this orthodox Pundit, who can still remain thus, in a mediæval atmosphere, antagonistic to many necessary reforms and blocking the way, time after time, to any further advance?

His importance surely lies in the fact that just because of his conservative character, with regard to all these articles of his own Hindu faith, he has kept touch with many millions of his fellow countrymen who are conservative also. He is unwilling to surrender the past at the imperious bidding of the modern age. He stands out for extreme simplicity of life: a diet which is bare almost to the limit of the ascetic, a supreme value set on the sanctity of marriage, a sense of the vastness of truth and right and harmlessness as the supreme things in religion. Those who know his own personal character, with its freedom from the baser passions, cannot help but feel that he is preserving something good. He is a model, in the modern age, of what the Brahman in ancient India aspired to be.

There is also one factor, which must always be taken into account, that comes out clearly in the story I have related above. In certain sudden emergencies, when the call of his country came to him with compelling force, he was ready to throw even his own strict Hindu ortho- doxy aside and take steps which led him into forbidden paths. Such a new step was taken when he decided to cross the sea and go to London in order to attend the Round Table Conference. Few in England can realise what a dramatic action that was. He would of course perform the necessary purifications after- wards; but it meant a very great deal, in his old age, when he had lived all the while in one atmosphere, suddenly to change the whole character of his daily life in such a novel manner. It may also

be said, to his credit, that with regard to the age of marriage, he *has* raised it voluntarily in his own family. What he objected to was any form of State compulsion which interfered with religion.

A danger, which Punditji himself had foreseen, has now loomed larger and larger, namely, the tension between Hin- duism and Islam. It may well be doubted whether the founding of the Hindu University at Benares has not increased that tension. While he has astonished the whole world by the way in which he has got the rich men of India to subscribe for the University, there has always been the hidden anxiety, beneath this outward success, lest its communal basis should increase the separation between the two religious cultures.

There have been very fine efforts made to save the Hindu University from

WITH HIS FAMILY
Pandit Malaviya with a group of his friends and relations at Benares.

such a fate, but the whole character of our times has tended to set the bias strongly in the sectarian direction; and in consequence the Aligarh University in the north-west of the United Provinces, and the Benares University in the south-east, have both been almost forced to become centres of propaganda for the two rival creeds, to the detriment of union and good-fellowship. What the future holds in store is very difficult to anticipate. Much will depend on Malaviyaji himself. But it would probably be true to say that the most dangerous feature in the life of modern India is this communal tension which has broken out again and again recently in riots ending in bloodshed and an increase of bitter hate.

With the advent of the Non-Cooperation Movement, the pathway forward of Pundit Madan Mohan Malaviya was strewn with difficulties. He had gone up, at the earliest possible moment, to the Punjab, in August, 1919, after the martial law had been withdrawn; and his account of what he had seen and heard, when he proclaimed it to the world, was the first direct information from a non-official source which had reached the world press and had become world news. He was able, also, to speak at length in the Legislative Council, at the Centre of the Government of India, in such a manner as to carry the conviction right home to the hearts of men that a terrible blunder, which was worse than a crime, had been committed. Above all, he made clear the humiliation, more shameful even than death, which had been forcibly imposed in Amritsar.

· But when the National Congress, under Mahatma Gandhi's leadership, had launched out on the full course of non-co-operation, his mind would not allow him to follow all the way. Above all, he was not ready to accept the Congress mandate with regard to the abandonment of the legislatures. He refused at the same time to leave the Congress; for he had an intense loyalty towards it as an institution which he had cherished from his youth up. He felt towards it a devotion which everyone deeply respected. When he stood out again and again, at the full Congress Sessions, and refused to vote in unison with the vast majority of delegates, he was always heard with the deepest respect and he retained in a very remarkable manner the affection of those who differed from him. But he could not change their own attitude towards Non-Co-operation; nor could they in the least degree alter his own fundamental ideas. Everyone knew that he would be the first to offer to go to prison, if his conscience would allow it: but his conscience for a long time did not move him in that direction. No one for a moment questioned his sincerity or his courage. In the end, however, he offered civil resistance and went to prison along with the rest.

There were probably two things which all the while moved him, subconsciously, though he would hardly think consciously about them. The former was his responsibility towards the Hindu University, which had received large emoluments from the Government of India. The second was his position, as the leading spirit in the Hindu Mahasabha, which also tied his hands to a considerable extent. He was not prepared that this whole communal organisation, containing many of the most eminent men in India, should be swung over to a definite position of antagonism to the Government.

Thus, while he had the utmost sympathy with the protest that was being made against what was called by Mahatma Gandhi "The Punjab Wrong" committed at Amritsar, and had condemned in the strongest manner the Government of India for not taking more drastic action against those who did the wrong, he was not prepared at first to go the whole length with Mahatmaji as to the method whereby the wrong should be set right. The fact that Non-Co-operation was succeeded very rapidly by the terrible Moplah Rising in the south, wherein many Hindus were brutally circumcised and thus "converted" to Islam in Malabar, made it impossible for him as an ardent Hindu to support the Khilafat Movement in the same whole-hearted way that Mahatma Gandhi did. Thus the conflict within his own soul became more and more acute, and he hardly knew, during the most anxious days in 1921 and 1922, where he stood.

No one was more pleased than Pundit Madan Mohan Malaviya when C. R. Das and Motilal Nehru broke away from the extreme form of Non-Co-operation and determined to fight the battle out *within* the Councils. But even here his own pathway was beset with difficulties. Pundit Motilal Nehru's position, as head of the Swaraj Party within the Congress, was not the same as his own. Motilal at the beginning was more determined on what were called "wrecking" tactics than was Malaviyaji himself, and he could never renounce the separate plat-form of his Hindu faith. Indeed, as we have seen, his Hinduism always occupied the first place in his mind, whenever the direct conflict came between Nationalism and Religion.

Added to this there was in him, as I have constantly discovered from my own experience of his inner mind, an intense belief in the liberalism expressed by Mr. Gladstone, whom he regarded as the greatest of all Englishmen in the nine-teenth century. This admiration con-tinually kept his mind dwelling rather on the "liberal" past than on the "socialist" future. Indeed, his whole idea of the Legislative Council at Simla and New Delhi was associated with that of the British Parliament in the great period when Gladstone was Prime Minister. He believed that it gave him a platform from which he could address the whole world; and so he prepared his speeches at various times with the utmost care. He had even a kind of reverence for the procedure of Parlia-ment which others did not share. He delivered his set speeches with an eloquence which was quite remarkable, when we consider the fact that the language he used was not his own mother tongue.

In a measure these large hopes were justified; for his speech delivered on behalf of the "Abolition of Inden-tured Labour," and that which I have already referred to on the "Punjab Disturbances," carried their full weight both inside and outside of the Council Chamber.

When Pundit Motilal Nehru came in at the head of the poll as the leader of the Swaraj Party everybody expected Pundit Madan Mohan Malaviya, as an old congress man, to join that party. But he decided instead to form one of his own, which was called the Nationalist Party. Malaviyaji's leadership was typically confined to Hindus. The strongest member under him was his old and trusted friend, Lala Lajpat Rai of the Punjab. When any vote of censure of Government bearing a national character was going to be proposed, both parties in the Assembly could be counted upon to vote together. In lesser matters, however, especially where some point that touched Hinduism was concerned, there was no such unanimity of opinion.

This constitutional attitude of what may be called responsive co-operation was broken at last by the events that happened in 1930. In that fateful year of non-co-operation Pundit Madan Mohan Malaviya at last broke through all his earlier self-imposed restraints and offered

himself again and again for imprisonment. I was not in India at the time
but the story reached me in America
how, after the arrest of Mahatma Gandhi
for breaking the Salt Act, a number of
new ordinances were passed and acts of
which everyone was afterwards ashamed
occurred during the *Lathi* charges in
Bombay. An extraordinary all-night
sitting of Malaviyaji, along with members
of the Working Committee, took place
in the streets of Bombay while the police
blocked their path and tried to move
them on. They, on their part, were
attempting to resist by non-violence

what they regarded as an arbitrary and
illegal order. During the years that
followed, in spite of his old age and the
immense respect that was paid to him
on every side, the Government of
India found it difficult to refrain from
imprisoning him and he was sentenced
many times over, but not for long
periods.

Of one of these imprisonments Jawaharlal Nehru wrote as follows:— "Pandit
Madan Mohan Malaviya was also transferred to Naini from some other gaol.
He was kept separately, not in our
barrack, but we met him daily, and

BENARES UNIVERSITY

*University College, Benares. Part of the great centre of Hindu culture, whose cause
Pandit Malaviya has done so much to further.*

perhaps I saw more of him there than I had done outside. He was a delightful companion, full of vitality and a youthful interest in things. He even started, with Ranjit's help, to learn German, and he showed quite a remarkable memory. He was in Naini when news of the floggings came, and he was greatly upset and wrote to the Acting-Governor of the Province. Soon afterwards he fell ill. He was unable to bear the cold in the conditions that prevailed in prison. His illness grew serious, and he had to be removed to the city hospital, and later to be discharged before his term was over. Happily, he recovered in hospital."

Again we find him arrested, along with Swarup Rani, Jawaharlal Nehru's mother, in 1933, but I cannot find out what happened after his arrest, or what sentence was passed. No one could have more bravely offered himself for imprisonment on all these occasions than Pundit Madan Mohan Malaviya.

It remains to try to sum in a few words his character, which all who have known him intimately have found so gentle and winning. No one, not even Mahatma Gandhi himself, is dearer to the vast majority of the Hindu public. He has also a great record of devotion to public national service, which places him very high indeed among those Indian leaders who are still living in our own times. There is in him a bravery of spirit which is equal to his tenderness of heart; and his religious faith is as simple as that of a child. Behind all is a personality so attractive that he has won the hearts of millions who have never even seen him, but have only known his great sacrifices both on behalf of his motherland and his Hindu faith.

BAL GANGADHAR TILAK

BAL GANGADHAR TILAK

"RESPECTED OF THE PEOPLE"

1856–1920

BY ROBERT BRYAN

THE period covered by the last decade of the nineteenth and the first decade of the twentieth centuries was marked in India by the growth of agitation in every sphere of life against the British rule and domination. Through the medium of the Indian-owned press, of the Indian National Congress, of the speeches and actions of Indians who visited or lived in England, of English people themselves like Charles Bradlaugh and later Mrs. Besant and C. F. Andrews, and, more reprehensibly, of the activities of terrorists in Bengal and the Bombay Presidency, the claims of Indians first to be associated on terms of equality in the government of their country, later to be granted home rule and a status equal to the self-governing portions of the British Empire, were ceaselessly and forcefully advanced. The force of this agitation took the Government of India, and many Indians as well, completely by surprise; it owed its origin and sustained continuance, more than to any other single factor, to the personality of Bal Gangadhar Tilak.

Before, however, the influence and the career of this remarkable man are discussed, it is necessary to get clear the background of past history against which he worked and which throughout his life so profoundly affected his thoughts. The crushing of the Indian Mutiny had led to a complete cessation of overt agitation against or dissatisfaction with British rule. Outwardly the years after 1858 were ones of internal peace. From open rebellion the British had nothing to fear. The Mutiny had,

however, left a feeling of bitterness in many Indian minds which neither time nor the British did much to dispel. The latter gave to Indians an efficient, but impersonal, administrative system, but only intermittent prosperity; a large measure of justice, but only in rare cases any real understanding; above all, remembering always the Mutiny, they tended to treat Indians not only as their inferiors but also as people who could not be trusted. It was not surprising that resentment persisted in the minds of educated Indians.

But whereas in the pre-Mutiny era— the heyday of the Brahmo-Samaj—the educated classes had been at one in embracing Western ideals, after 1858 they split into two camps, of which one maintained that though Western education should be utilised to the full, yet all that was best in thought and action was contained in the tenets of orthodox Hinduism. This point of view was typified by the Arya Samaj and the "Back to the Vedas" movement, its upholders execrated the · foreigners ("mlecchas"), displayed a harsh intolerance towards everything that was not Hindu; pre-eminent among them, at least during the early years of his prominence, was Tilak, though it is one of his main claims to greatness that he moved finally a considerable distance from this attitude.

Bal Gangadhar Tilak was born at Ratnagiri on the Konkan Coast in 1856. He was by birth a Brahman, which was to be an important factor in his life, and the sect to which he belonged was the Chitpavan, which was the predominant influence controlling his early activities. The Chitpavan Brahmans had been in the 18th and the early part of the 19th centuries *de facto* rulers of the Maratha kingdom, which had its capital at Poona —and the resistance of the Marathas to the English power had been at once more skilfully conducted, more stubborn and more prolonged than that of any other Indian kingdom, Hindu or Moslem. Towards their alien English rulers who had deprived them of their power and pre-eminence many of them felt an animosity more bitter, sustained and purposeful than was to be found anywhere else in India.

Tilak was brought up in the strictly orthodox Brahman tradition: as a Chitpavan he had behind him a tradition of politics and public service; as a Maratha he was told the stories of the glorious days of Shivaji and the Maratha Empire, the days when "the foreigners"—in this case the Moslems—were driven in ignominy from Maharashtra. He went as a young man to Poona, the centre of Maratha irredentism, where, as soon after the Mutiny as 1862, an abortive conspiracy had sought to re-establish the power of the Peshwas. There he was appointed professor of mathematics in the New English School, and there, after a while, he became the founder and proprietor of two journals, the *Maratha*, printed in English, and the *Kesari*. The latter, which was the first one printed in a vernacular—Marathi—to gain any noticeable circulation among educated Indians, was destined to gain fame throughout the peninsula. Hitherto education and day-to-day information had been assimilated through the medium of the English tongue. Tilak's earliest ideal—to which he gave practical expression by helping to found National Schools independent of government control, which, however, were later suppressed—was that English should

take second place to, if not altogether be supplanted by, the vernacular in the sphere of education as well as of the press.

When Tilak was twenty-nine years old the first session of the Indian National Congress was being held in Bombay. Presided over by an Englishman, Allan Hume, regarded with benevolence as something harmless by the Viceroy, Lord Dufferin, it was mildly liberal in tone and nowhere expressed hostility to the British connection. Tilak was not present at this first meeting, though he had already made his mark in the Bombay Presidency. Violent in speech and print, he had already, in the Poona Sarvajanik Sabha and the Education Committee of which he and Ranade were the leading lights, proved himself the intolerant champion of Hinduism, often in a reactionary form.

He was, however, a delegate to the fifth session of the Congress at Bombay in 1889. His speeches in this and succeeding sessions, particularly his demand that the attitude of "mendicancy," the habit of begging favours from the British, should be abandoned, did much to drive Congress into opposition to the established government; his famous cry, "Freedom is my birthright, and I will have it," awoke an emotional echo throughout India. His attitude, however, aroused misgivings among many of the Moderates. Ranade, and later even Gokhale and Surendrenath Banerjea, not only viewed with alarm the violence of his language but also began to suspect that he spoke and acted first as a Brahman, second as a Maratha, and only incidentally as a man with a vision of a united India of the future.

It must be admitted that his actions, during the closing years of the nineteenth century, did much to justify these suspicions. In 1890 the Government of India introduced the Age of Consent Bill, forbidding the consummation of a marriage before the wife was twelve years old. Its provisions commanded assent from all those who clung to the ideals of the Brahmo Samaj, but Tilak, the orthodox Brahman, violently opposed it. His attitude won him praise from strictly orthodox Hindus, who abounded in Maharashtra, and from all those who welcomed any gesture of defiance to the British. Through the columns of the *Kesari*—which was to attain the then altogether remarkable circulation of 20,000 copies—he could already address a large public, and his personality, as well as the note of challenge and defiance in his writings and speeches, brought him an immense and unquestioning following. Outstanding in intellect, subtle as well as forceful in argument, he could rouse in those with whom he came into contact the same violent emotions, whether of enthusiasm or hatred, which he himself felt. On any given issue he was passionately sincere and he had the gift that was to be later pre-eminently Gandhi's, of inspiring unquestioning devotion. He was given, by common consent, the name of Lokamanya, "respected by the people."

Tilak in these early years bent all his efforts to re-awake in the Maratha people a sense of their past greatness with a view to future independence. He went among the poor villagers of the Deccan as well as the townspeople of Poona, urging the revival of celebrations in connexion with Ganpati, the elephant-headed God known to every village in India, and in 1893 he organised in Poona the first public festival in the God's honour. He founded Ganpati Societies, banded the students in the towns and the youths in the villages into *melas* and gymnastic societies, giving to them a corporate feeling and a sense of their own importance, the while he urged them in the columns of the *Kesari* to

deeds of self-denial and valour—and by implication, violence—in defence of their ancient glory against the hated foreigner. In the same year he founded the Anti-Cow-Killing Society, a direct challenge to Moslems which he followed up by demanding, at meetings of the Sarvajanik Sabha, from the Government the lifting of the ban on the playing of music by Hindu processions in front of mosques. As a result the Moslem members of the Sabha resigned, but Tilak acquired fresh popularity as the champion of the Hindus.

Further to consolidate Maratha sentiment and activity Tilak determined to revive the worship of the greatest of all Maratha heroes, Shivaji, the founder of the Maratha power. In 1895 he organised and presided over the first great Shivaji festival at Raigarh, Shivaji's first capital. There was recited by one of Tilak's followers a poem written specially for the occasion, the sense of which was as follows:

"Let us be prompt like Shivaji to engage in desperate enterprises. Take up your swords and shields and we shall cut off countless heads of enemies. Listen! Though we shall have to risk our lives in a national war, we shall assuredly shed the life-blood of our enemies."

There also Tilak himself spoke. In Shivaji's life there had been one incident —the killing with the notorious "tiger's claw" of Afzul Khan, the opposing general with whom he was in peace-conference—which laid him open to the charge of treachery. Tilak's way of treating the incident was highly significant.

"It is needless to make further researches into the killing of Afzul Khan. Let us even assume that Shivaji deliberately planned and executed the murder. . . . Did Shivaji commit a sin in killing Afzul Khan?

The answer to this question can be found in the Mahabharata itself. The divine Krishna teaching in the Gita tells us we may kill even our teachers and our kinsmen, and no blame. attaches if we are not actuated by selfish desires. . . . God has conferred on the foreigners no grant of Hindustan inscribed on imperishable brass. Shivaji strove to drive them forth out of the land of his birth, but he was guiltless of the sin of covetousness. Do not circumscribe your vision like frogs in a well. Rise above the Penal Code into the rarefied atmosphere of the sacred Bhagavad Gita and consider the action of great men."

There could be no clearer incitement to violent action, no clearer indication of that policy of condoning, if not actually inspiring, assassination, which he was shortly to adopt.

The years 1896 and 1897 were marked by an appalling famine not only in the Deccan but throughout India. Tilak was untiring and selfless in his efforts to relieve the distress, but neither voluntary service nor the measures which the various administrations were able to put into effect prevented untold suffering and a heavy mortality rate. Widespread bitterness was felt at the inability of the British to do more, and this bitterness was increased tenfold by the first outbreak, in Bombay Presidency in 1897, of bubonic plague in India. Once again Tilak displayed great energy and unselfishness. He refused to leave Poona, where the disease was raging and whence many who could afford to had fled, and organized relief on a wide scale. He worked through the Sarvajanik Sabha—with whom the British authorities unwisely refused to co-operate— and started Hindu Plague Hospitals throughout the city. At the same time he carried on a series of bitter attacks on

the British in the *Kesari*. The measures which officials had to take to combat the plague ran counter to many Hindu religious customs and inborn prejudices. Tilak took full advantage of this, accusing the administration not only of incompetence but of deliberate and unnecessary interference in matters that good Hindus held sacred. Utterly sincere in his hatred of British domination, he was careless of what means he employed to achieve his end, and he inflamed the sentiments of his listeners and readers to a dangerously explosive emotional point.

In June, 1897, two British officials, Rand and Ayerst, were assassinated in Poona by a young Chitpavan, Damodar Chapekar. There is no shred of evidence that Tilak either planned the assassination or directly incited the assassin, but the deed was the inevitable consequence on an emotional youth of the tone of his articles in the *Kesari*. On account of these articles he was prosecuted for sedition, convicted on a majority vote of six European jurors against three Indians, and sentenced to eighteen months' imprisonment.

The murder of Rand and Ayerst is a landmark in Indian history for two reasons. It marked the start of organised terrorism and it resulted, owing to his subsequent conviction, in the final emergence of Tilak as a popular hero. His term of imprisonment was widely regarded as a martyrdom in the cause of Indian freedom and on his release he became at once the leader of the extremist party in Congress. For that position he was eminently fitted, for no single man had done more in the previous years to awaken in Indians, educated and uneducated, the desire to govern themselves and the feeling that they were fitted so to do. In its early days Congress had been mainly a body of intellectuals thinking in terms of the intellect. Tilak had been the first Indian to bring political agitation to the masses; now after the famine and the plague, which had affected not only Maharashtra, but the whole of India, the time was ripe to direct their thoughts into anti-British channels. Tilak was not the man to lose the opportunity.

Between moderate Congressmen like Naoroji, Gokhale and Surendrenath Banerjea and Tilak and his two chief allies, Bepin Chandra Pal and Arabindo Ghose there was always fundamental agreement on the end to be achieved, the governing of India by Indians. That Tilak was now recognised as more than a champion of orthodox Maratha Brahmanism is proved by his close collaboration with Bepin Chandra Pal, a Bengali of convinced reformist views. But upon the way of achievement the two wings of Congress came increasingly to differ. Hating violence, bearing no animosity against individual Englishmen, the Moderates were opposed to terrorism in all its forms. Tilak, on the other hand, who had become secretary of the Standing Committee for the Deccan, maintained that discussion and the passing of resolutions would achieve nothing, that only by direct action could they hope to achieve their goal—and by direct action he meant the use of the boycott weapon and the encouragement of political assassination. His ideas, which had already found acceptance in the Deccan, took root now even more effectively in Bengal, which took and in future held the lead in terrorist activities. To some extent the Government of India played into the extremists' hands; the partition of Bengal in 1905, against the clearly expressed wishes of its inhabitants, strengthened Tilak's position. To the demand for *Swadeshi*—which he had earlier put forward to Congress—he now added a demand for the complete boycott of British goods.

At the Congress meeting at Benares in 1905 the principle of the boycott was partially accepted; in 1906 at Calcutta the President, Dadabhai Naoroji, himself a Moderate, spoke more firmly than ever before. "We do not ask for any favours, we want only justice . . . the whole matter can be comprised in one word—"self-government" or "Swaraj." It was the standpoint taken up by Tilak many years before. The tone of this presidential speech, however, raised false hopes that the Moderates might in the following year adopt the full boycott policy, with all that it might entail. At Surat, where Congress assembled in 1907, it became obvious at once that no such change of heart had taken place. A violent scene developed, Surendrenath Banerjea being constantly interrupted by Tilak's party, and the second day Congress broke up in confusion. Not for ten years was Tilak, or those who thought with him, to attend its meetings.

The split in the Congress ranks that occurred at Surat was a blow to the ideal of Indian unity; a main factor contributing to it was Tilak's own uncompromising attitude. At Surat there was a dangerous recrudescence of the cleavage between Maharashtra and the rest of India. But neither his break with Congress nor the civil and criminal proceedings in which in the previous years he had been involved, did anything to lessen his popularity. In the Tai Maharaj case he was accused, as an executor, of forgery, perjury and corruption. On the criminal proceedings he was at first found guilty, but on appeal the conviction was set aside. In the civil proceedings brought against him on the same issue three trials were necessary, but again finally, before the Privy Council sitting in London, judgment was given in his favour. In the political field he had found a new outlet for his activities in the mill-hands of

Bombay. Miserably housed and miserably paid, they reacted at once to his propaganda which once again was compounded of disinterestedness—as in his efforts to curb the evils of drunkenness—and hatred of the British. That he, an orthodox Brahman, should condescend to come among the poor millhands, should strive to better their conditions, was a thing to make them wonder and then worship, and in his controversy with the Moderates it was he whom they regarded as their champion.

In the meantime he continued his control of the *Kesari*, which had now found many imitators throughout India, and it was again one of his articles therein that for a second time caused him to be tried, convicted and imprisoned. In 1908 Mrs. and Miss Kennedy were killed in Bengal by a bomb thrown by a terrorist. Tilak in the *Kesari* applauded the latter's action, comparing it with that of Chapekar eleven years earlier and praising both. The article was clearly intended to be an incitement to further similar deeds and Tilak, despite a speech in his own defence that lasted for $21\frac{1}{2}$ hours, was sentenced to six years' transportation; this was commuted to imprisonment at Mandalay. Such was Tilak's popularity, that riots, breaking out in Bombay after news of the sentence, continued for six days.

With his imprisonment the most important part of his career was ended. He had already done more than any other man to raise active opposition to the British, first in Maharashtra, then in Bengal, and in lesser degree throughout the rest of India. He has been called "the Father of Indian Unrest," and the title is an apt one. As such he had come to enjoy immense popularity and prestige among Hindus of all castes. He had become something much more

than a Maratha leader. When his term of imprisonment was over, though he was past middle age and had lived a turbulent life, he resumed many of his former activities. He found a new and powerful ally in Mrs. Annie Besant, and in 1915 formed a Home Rule League. In 1916 he attended, for the first time for ten years, the annual session of the Congress, held at Lucknow. The tone of that session, in the course of which the Moderates and the Extremists joined in demanding from the British an announcement that "it is the aim and intention of British policy to confer self-government on India at an early date," was the predominant cause of the introduction of the reforms embodied in the Government of India Act of 1919. The prestige of Congress was immensely strengthened by the return of Tilak; it is at least possible that if there had been no reconciliation, the British Government might have ignored its demands, or that the demands would not have been made.

After the armistice Tilak took a leading part in demanding that India should be represented on terms of equality with the other Dominions at the Peace Conference, and in anticipation of this he was chosen by Congress, together with Mr. Gandhi and Syed Hasan Imam, as a delegate thereto. When the British Government refused to grant him a passport, he wrote to M. Clemenceau, Premier of France and President of the Peace Conference, claiming that "with her (India's) vast area, enormous resources, and prodigious population, she may well aspire to be a leading power in Asia, if not in the world. She could therefore be a powerful steward of the League of Nations in the East for maintaining the peace of the world and the stability of the British Empire against all aggressors and disturbers of peace whether in Asia or elsewhere." India,

Tilak would in fact maintain, as at this time did Gandhi, aspired to freedom, but freedom as a partner in the British Empire.

In 1919 Tilak did visit England as the leading member of a deputation sent by Congress to put its point of view with regard to the new Government of India Act. Tilak appeared before the Joint Select Committee of Parliament, and was active in reorganising the British Committee of the Congress so that it could more effectively put the Congress point of view before the British public. He became involved in a libel action against Sir Valentine Chirol who had, after Tilak's imprisonment in 1908, published some severe strictures on him in *The Times*, which were reprinted in book form. It was after losing this action that he returned to India.

He was still a force in Indian political life, though events had moved far from the days of the *Kesari*. He himself had broadened and mellowed in outlook. By taking a leading part in bringing about the Lucknow Pact with the Moslem League in 1916 he had shown that he no longer classed Moslems as "foreigners," and he incited his followers no more to violence. But though a force, he was no longer the chief force, in Indian Nationalism; his mantle as a popular leader rested on the shoulders of Mahatma Gandhi. At the Amritsar Congress in 1919, which both attended, it was to Gandhi that members looked for leadership. In 1920 Congress adopted Gandhi's plan of non-violent non-co-operation; August 1 was the day fixed for the putting into practice of the new principle of *Satayagraha*, a principle so alien to the temperament of at least the Tilak of earlier years. On that same day, the day on which Gandhi arrived in the city, Tilak died in Bombay. A vast crowd, which included Gandhi and Jawaharlal Nehru, followed the funeral procession.

It is, frankly, difficult for an Englishman to form a just estimate of the measure of Tilak's greatness; though in his later years he grew more moderate, he had, through all the most active years of his life, been ruthless in his hatred of British rule, and it is not easy for a member of that race to condone the acts of terrorism in the Deccan and Bengal which he did so much to inspire. Yet that there were elements of real greatness in his character is not to be denied. He was, in fact, much more than a politician: he was a leader. Many aspects of his leadership were deplored not only by the British but also by many of his fellow Indians who were just as disinterested as he in the service of their country, but this salient fact remains: more than any man of his generation he was the cause of the great re-awakening of self-respect and self-confidence that came to India in the years before the war, and in his later years he was a powerful factor in the creation of an All-India opinion.

It must be held greatly to Tilak's credit that he, who in the nineteenth century could do his utmost to inflame Hindu opinion against the Moslems, should be a prime mover in effecting the considerable step forward towards Hindu-Moslem unity marked by the Lucknow Pact. After his death his great successor in the public esteem, Mahatma Gandhi, strove ceaselessly to the same end. Between the methods used by these two men to establish a free India there is a wide gulf fixed; to Gandhi the use of bullet, dagger or bomb is anathema. Yet this they have in common: to both was accorded by millions in India a hero-worship which is only given to those who, according to their lights, are doing their utmost to ensure the greatness of their country.

SIR SURENDRANATH BANERJEA

SIR SURENDRANATH BANERJEA

AWAKENER OF INDIAN POLITICAL CONSCIOUSNESS
1848–1925

BY SIR VERNEY LOVETT, K.C.S.I., M.A. (Oxon)

SURENDRANATH BANERJEA was born in 1848, the year in which Lord Dalhousie became Governor-General, six years before the Educational Despatch of Sir Charles Wood laid the foundations of a great change in the government of India, and nine years before the outbreak of the Mutiny. His grandfather was an orthodox Kulin Brahman of Calcutta; his father was a doctor who had studied Western medicine in the first Calcutta Medical College. He tells us in his Autobiography[1] that at his home "Eastern orthodoxy and Western culture strove together for mastery." The grandfather was predominant as long as he lived; but the father saw that his son was educated on Western lines and sent him to a school founded mainly by the generosity of Captain Doveton of the Nizam's service and attended chiefly by Anglo-Indian pupils. He matriculated at the Calcutta University, which had been established only a few years before, at the age of fifteen, and studied hard with the assistance of Anglo-Indian and European professors and teachers to whom in after years he expressed warm gratitude. While a student he was attracted by the addresses of Keshub Chandar Sen of the Brahmo Samaj to whom he listened with "ever increasing admiration," perceiving "the power of oratory over the Indian mind." His father attended to his physical as well as to his mental development. He ascribes the exceptional health enjoyed by members of his family "to the absence of child marriage for many years among them."

[1] *A Nation in Making*—1925.

When he took his B.A. degree, by the advice of the Principal of his College his father decided to send him to England to compete for the Indian Civil Service. But in spite of the paternal approval, the enterprise required considerable courage. "I started," he writes, "with Romesh Chandar Dutt and Bihari Lal Gupta. We were all young, in our teens, and a visit to England was a more serious affair than it is now. It not only meant absence from home and those near and dear to me for a number of years but there was the grim prospect of social ostracism, which for all practical purposes has now happily passed away. We all three had to make our arrangements in secret, as if we were engaged in some nefarious plot of which the world should know nothing." In such circumstances Indian competition was naturally negligible and confined entirely to a few youths from the then very limited classes that had turned to English education, the commercial, medical, legal and clerical professions in the sea-port towns, mostly Hindus. Surendranath and his two friends passed the Open Competition of 1869 and proceeded to a probationary period in the University of London. He writes with much appreciation of its professors and teachers and of the hospitable and kindly treatment that the three received. They passed out at the Final Examination of 1871, and travelling leisurely over Europe sailed by an Italian steamer for Bombay and arrived at Calcutta in September 1871. A big reception was held in their honour in a public garden, but they had still to contend with conservative Hindu prejudice, and Surendranath's family was at first "practically outcasted" for receiving him. Perhaps if his enlightened father had been alive, things would have been easier, but he had died during Surendranath's absence in England. His stay in Calcutta was short, as he was posted to Sylhet as Assistant Magistrate and Collector in November, 1871. After a brief career under a District Officer whom he found unsympathetic he fell into trouble over the trial of a case and was reported to the High Court and the Bengal Government. The matter was, under the rules, investigated by a special commission of three senior officers whose report was unfavourable; and eventually he was dismissed by the Secretary of State in Council on the recommendation of the Government of India with a compassionate allowance of Rs50 per month. He tells his own story and supports it by quoting the opinion of A. O. Hume, "the father of the Indian National Congress." There was, of course, the government side to it. But it all happened nearly seventy years ago and the full circumstances cannot be adjudicated on now.

He had presented himself in London to plead his own cause and on being informed of the verdict decided to return to India as a barrister. During his previous stay in England he had kept eight terms at the Middle Temple. He continued to eat his dinners, but in 1875 the Benchers declined to call him to the Bar as he had been dismissed from the Indian Civil Service. This was a heavy blow, and he writes that he felt that he had suffered as an Indian, "a member of a community that lay disorganised, that had no public opinion, and no voice in the counsels of their government." There can be no doubt that this idea influenced his subsequent career. During the whole of his stay in England he studied hard, reading books which he

thought would assist him to become instrumental in promoting an altered state of things. He returned to India in June, 1875, and beginning as Professor of English in the Metropolitan Institution gradually rose in the educational world of Calcutta, attaining great influence among the students to whom he lectured upon such subjects as Indian Unity, the study of History, the life of Mazzini and the life of Chaitanya.[1] He had resolved to stir them out of their indifference to politics "while protecting them from extreme fanatical views," and with this object he assisted in the organisation of a Students' Association. He further became a very active member of the new "Indian Association" established in July, 1876, by advanced members of the Calcutta middle class of Hindus with the idea of eventually bringing all India upon a common political platform. Its ideals were (1) the creation of a strong body of public opinion in the country; (2) the unification of the Indian races upon the basis of common political interests; (3) the promotion of friendly feelings between Hindus and Moslems; (4) the inclusion of the masses in public movements. Prominent among its members, Surendranath travelled into provinces outside Bengal developing his unusual oratorical talent, and discovering that "a common system of administration had prepared the ground for the realisation of one of our most cherished ideals, namely, united action by the different Indian provinces for the fulfilment of our national aims and aspirations."

I have followed Surendranath Banerjea through his formative years, and have shown the main influences to which his eager, impressionable character was subjected. It must be remembered that under the legislation of 1861 India was then governed by a Governor-General in Council on which no Indian

[1] A Hindu poet and saint.

sat, that Indians were not represented on any provincial executive Council, that for legislation not less than six nor more than twelve additional members were summoned to assist the central Executive, not less than half of whom were non-officials. As railways, education, commerce, roads, contact with Europe increased, it was inevitable that English-educated Indians should ask for a larger share in the government of the country. But the English view was that for good government, and for the general content of all the many sections of an enormous society of varied races and religions, it was impossible to abdicate effective control; or to delegate to any class or minority the duty of providing for so vast a congerie of peoples "marching in uneven stages through all the centuries from the fifth to the twentieth."[1] Politically-minded Indians were as yet few in number and mainly Hindu, but with spreading education and persistent agitation they began to increase among the English-educated professional class. Surendranath gradually became conspicuous as a vehement agitator. His influence was increased by his opposition to the Vernacular Press Act of 1878, passed by Lord Lytton's Government and repealed by Lord Ripon's, as well as by his tours in country districts to stimulate interest in Lord Ripon's local self-government policy—intended not with a view to improvement in administration but "as a measure of political and popular education." He tells us that the Indian Association regarded this measure as a first stepping-stone to a demand for a representative government. By this time he had become editor and proprietor of the *Bengalee* which he converted from an insignificant weekly into a successful daily newspaper. Civil imprisonment for two months for contempt of Court, at the time when the Ilbert Bill contro-

versy was agitating Calcutta, increased the popularity which it is evident that he greatly enjoyed. After the Legislative Councils were enlarged in 1892 by an Act which recognised the elective principle he was elected to the Bengal Council and sat on it for eight years from 1893 to 1901, representing three different constituencies. He very strongly opposed the 1899 bill for reforming and " officialising" the Calcutta Corporation in conformity with the views of Lord Curzon, and refused to sit further on that body when this measure became law.

In the meantime the Indian National Congress had for some years recognised Surendranath as one of its leading members and appointed him to its deputation to England in 1890. It remain.. d essentially and mainly a Hindu body. The great Moslem leader, Sir Saiyid Ahmad, had warned his co-religionists that a parliamentary system would subject them to the predominantly numerous Hindus, and that loyalty to Britain was their soundest policy. Within the circle of the Congress leaders there was difference of opinion as to the participation of students in politics. Surendranath favoured this idea, holding that students might even "take part in political work, subject to proper control and guidance." As we shall see, he afterwards acted on this principle vigorously in the agitation against the partition of Bengal; but after that and subsequent experiences, writing on the subject in his last years, he observed that while he still held his former views, "some of our young men have displayed an unpardonable intolerance of views opposed to their own"; there have been "demonstrations of rowdiness." Although "discipline is the soul of student life," its bonds had been relaxed and a spirit of disorder was gaining ground. He could only hope that this would be a

[1] *Lord Morley.*

9*

temporary and passing phase. But in those earlier years he continued to lecture and speak as an educationist and politician. He remarks: "My professional work greatly helped me in my public speeches as I had to teach the classics of the English language. Among them were the speeches and writings of Burke, Froude, Lord Morley and others. I thus lived in · constant association with the great masters of the English language and in close familiarity with their vocabulary and methods of thought, and to none do I owe a greater debt than Edmund Burke, whose political philosophy has so largely moulded my own views about government and society."

But with the advent of Bal Gangadhar Tilak into the Congress leading circles came a strong wind of reactionary Hinduism from Western India, and the beginnings of political extremism. Nowhere did Tilak's methods and organisations attract more attention than in Bengal. This was plainly to be seen later on in the anti-partition agitation. On July 26, 1899, before Lord Curzon had been a year in the country he observed in a private letter[1]—"There is no doubt that a sort of quasi-metaphysical ferment is going on in India, strongly conservative and even reactionary in its general tendency. The ancient philosophies are being re-exploited and their modern scribes and professors are increasing in number and fame. What is to come out of this strange amalgam—with European ideas thrown as an outside ingredient into the crucible—who can say?" As Lord Ronaldshay writes, "Curzon turned from these insoluble problems of the spirit to the more pressing problems of administration, to which it was no idle boast to say that he habitually devoted ten hours out of every twenty-four." Yet, curiously enough, he largely underrated the

[1] *Ronaldshay, II, p. 199.*

potential influence of the Congress, and even as late as December, 1900, believed that it was "tottering to its fall," and represented only a small section of the community. But in those days the wars and disturbing world-developments of the new century were hidden from the eyes of us all. Three acts of Curzon's government were particularly repugnant to Surendranath and other leaders of the Congress: the curtailment of the power of the elected element on the Calcutta Corporation, already referred to; the Universities Bill, which came too late and ran too sharply against popular prejudices and vested interests to effect much real improvement; and last but not least the partition of the old overgrown province of Bengal, Bihar and Orissa in such a manner as to split Bengal itself into halves, an operation which synchronised with the close of the Russo-Japanese war. In each of these bitter controversies Surendranath took a prominent part, and encouraged students and schoolboys to take part in picketing during the boycott movement. The results were lamentable and far-reaching. The whole boycott movement exacerbated Hindu and Moslem relations to an extreme degree in Eastern Bengal, and when at last Surendranath began to perceive the error of his ways, enormous mischief had been done. A significant incident is related on pp. 223–4 of his autobiography. He was approached by two young men with a proposal to shoot Sir Bamfylde Fuller, the Lieutenant-Governor of the new province of Eastern Bengal and Assam, because of a newspaper story. He deterred them from the idea and about this time awoke to the fact that the agitation was covering the operations of thorough-going revolutionaries. There is a note of personal reminiscence in some of the last words which he addressed to his countrymen (*in A Nation Making*—p. 402): "Talk not of revolutions, or of tactics, such as obstruction, which are allied to revolutionary movements. You would then stand upon a dangerous precipice and might be hurried, despite yourselves, into the abysmal depths of a real revolutionary movement with all the terrible consequences, the bloodshed and the reaction that follow in its train. Pray do not play with fire. When a movement has been set on foot, forces gather round it of which perhaps you had not the faintest conception, and impart to it a volume and momentum beyond the ideas of the originators who are now powerless to control it."

At Surat, in 1907, he took a leading part in preventing the Extremists from dominating the Congress; and when in 1909 his friend Ashutosh Biswas, public prosecutor, was murdered by a revolutionary he spoke in the Calcutta Town Hall in strong denunciation of the crime. The split at Surat between Moderates and Extremists had left the Moderates in possession of the Congress. They had declared its objective to be self-government within the Empire, to be obtained by constitutional means. They accepted the Minto-Morley reforms which a Bengali deputation to the Viceroy pronounced to be "a step worthy of the noble traditions of the Government which has given us liberty of thought and speech, high education and good government." The most prominent moderate leaders were in Bengal, Surendranath, and in Western India, Gopal Krishna Gokhale. But even by Moderates in Bengal the partition was still denounced, and on the stream of revolutionary crime the reforms produced no effect. A confederacy of revolutionary conspirators drew its recruits from the schools and colleges of Bengal and, in spite of a Press Act passed in 1910, was encouraged by the tone of some newspapers. In 1911 came the

visit of King George V and Queen Mary to India, which was a brilliant success and distinctly influenced the general attitude of the country on the outbreak of the War. At the Coronation Durbar of December, 1911, it was announced that the partition of Bengal would be modified in such a manner as to leave that province intact, and that the capital of India would be moved from Calcutta to Delhi. But revolutionary conspiracy did not cease in Bengal even in August, 1914, when princes, politicians and people rallied strongly to the Empire's cause. As one who witnessed and rejoiced in the unity of those days, I can testify to its reality. When the Imperial Legislative Council passed with eager unanimity a resolution of "unswerving loyalty and enthusiastic devotion to their King-Emperor and unflinching support to the British Government," Surendranath said: "We aspire to colonial self-government, then we ought to emulate the example of the Colonials and try to do what they are doing."

But with the long strain of the War and the Home Rule Movement led by Mrs. Besant and Tilak came a certain political reaction. The Congress and the Moslem League, the latter largely moved by pro-Turkish influences, held simultaneous meetings at Lucknow in December, 1916, and each declared for colonial self-government, agreeing on separate electorates for the Mohammedans. In these consultations Surendranath took a prominent part. The Moderates had, to their subsequent embarrassment, readmitted the Extremists into the Congress fold. Later on, in August, 1917, came the declaration of a new policy by the Secretary of State for India—"increasing associations of Indians in every branch of administration; and the gradual development of self-governing institutions, with a view to the progressive realisation of responsible government in India as an integral part of the British Empire." The visit of Mr. Montagu eventuated in the publication of the Montagu-Chelmsford proposals for wide constitutional reforms which immediately produced a definite and lasting split between political Moderates and Extremists. The former left the Congress; the latter remained in possession. In the Viceroy's Legislative Council Surendranath Banerjea, as leader of the Moderates, moved a resolution approving generally of the new proposals, subject to minor criticisms, and inviting his countrymen to "grasp with alacrity and enthusiasm the hand of fellowship and friendship held out to them and in co-operation with British statesmen to move forward to those high destinies which, under the Providence of God, are reserved for our people." The resolution was carried with only two dissentients; and Surendranath justly claims that it saved the new scheme. I was present on this occasion and felt that the attitude of the non-official members was one of genuine cordiality. A resolution moved by a non-official member recommending that consideration and disposal of the Report of the Sedition (Rowlatt) Committee be kept in abeyance was rejected by 46 to 2 votes. But these fair beginnings of a new era were, as is well known, marred by much that followed. It is sufficient here to say that although Surendranath and the other Moderate members of the Imperial Legislative Council opposed the anti-revolutionary conspiracies legislation of February and March, 1919, yet when bitter agitation outside the Council increased and Mr. Gandhi inaugurated the policy of civil disobedience by communicating to the Press a pledge signed by himself and others, the Moderates countered by a manifesto expressing disapproval of this innovation. It was pointed out in one of their newspapers that the principle involved in the proposed pledge was extremely dangerous and might lead anywhere. The bill passed; the riots of April, 1919, and severe repression followed; and shortly afterwards Surendranath spent four months in England in order to attend the sittings of the Joint Parliamentary Committee that was considering the Government of India Bill of 1919. He returned in September but received a somewhat chilly welcome from his old followers. "Non-co-operation," he says, "had done its work by creating a profound sense of mistrust in British promises and pledges among a certain section of our people despite evidence of earnest efforts to redeem them." He notes that when it became clear to its authors that non-co-operation was marked by unrest and rowdyism and sometimes by bloodshed, that it achieved nothing constructive, it was converted into a policy of entry into the reformed Councils for the purpose of obstructing and wrecking them. This policy he strongly opposed. At a meeting of the Rotary Club in Calcutta he appealed to the members "to stand with us, to co-operate with us in ensuring the success of the great experiment upon which the honour of England is staked, and the future of India so largely depends. I am sure," he added, "that I do not appeal in vain. I am strengthened in this note by the cordiality of your reception and the kind and sympathetic hearing which you have accorded to me and for which I am truly grateful." He certainly did not appeal in vain.

He was knighted on January 1, 1921, and became a Minister in the Reformed Provincial Executive Council, accepting the portfolio of local self-government and the medical department. He writes warmly of his relations with the Governor, Lord Ronaldshay, with his colleagues in the government, both Hindu and Moslem, and with the Services, of the loyal help which he received from his secretary, Mr. O'Malley. He quotes the letter "of great regret in severing connection" which he received from the Surgeon-General of Bengal when his term of office came to a close in January, 1924.

But there was another side to the picture which he describes in language of sorrow. "The Press of Bengal was saturated with the spirit of non-co-operation and was Extremist in its views and utterances. The reception accorded to us was cold and hostile." Even friendly critics expected impossibilities, not recognising that "the work in its most difficult and controversial aspects necessarily resolved itself into a series of compromises." He framed and passed on March 7, 1923, a new Calcutta Municipal Act which superseded the Act passed by Lord Curzon in 1899, and restored supreme authority over the affairs of the City to the Corporation, four-fifths of whose members were to be elected by the ratepayers. Both the Mayor and the chief executive officer were to be its nominees, subject only to confirmation by the government. Surendranath calls the measure "a veritable Swaraj in the government of the second city of the Empire," and in the Provincial Legislative Council appealed for co-operation for its success. "Let no party spirit," he said, "mar the fruition of this great object." The new Corporation, however, was captured by his Swarajist adversaries, and his bitterest opponent became Mayor. At the Council election of 1923 he was defeated and practically excluded from public affairs for the rest of his life. He expresses, however, his faith that eventually a civic government will be established in Calcutta "not for the benefit of a party or clique but for the benefit of the people and worked through the people."

On retiring from office he finished his Memoirs and died on August 6, 1925. His memoirs are of great interest for they are a very human document and show clearly the ambitions and principles which guided his public life. He goes out of his way to pay warm tribute to old friends and colleagues and to some of the masters of English literature from whose writings he derived so much inspiration. His tone towards old antagonists is generally void of bitterness. We see the ideas that animated his political strivings, sometimes carrying him further than he cares directly to admit. "For self-government," he says, "I have worked step by step, stage by stage. I worked for it when the government treated it as a fantastic dream. Our efforts have changed all this, and even the view-point of the government. The message of August 20, 1917, is the tribute to our success." He ends by pleading earnestly with his countrymen for a policy of co-operation. "There is no standing still in this world of God's providence. Move on we must with eyes reverently fixed on the past, with a loving concern for the present, and with deep solicitude for the future. We must in this onward journey assimilate from all sides into our character, our culture, our civilisation, whatever is suited to our genius and is calculated to strengthen and invigorate it and weave it into the texture of our national life. Thus, co-operation and not non-co-operation, assimilation and not isolation must be a living and growing factor in the evolution of our people. Any other policy would be suicidal and fraught with peril to our best interests. That is my message to my countrymen, delivered not in haste or impatience, but as the mature result of my deliberations and of my life-long labours in the service of the Motherland."

CHITTA RANJAN DAS

CHITTA RANJAN DAS

THE FRIEND OF HIS COUNTRY
1870–1925

BY DR. J. C. GHOSH

CHITTA RANJAN DAS, political leader, lawyer, poet and journalist, was born on the 5th of November, 1870, in Calcutta. He was the eldest son of Bhuban Mohan Das and Nistarini Devi. The Das family was one of the most distinguished and cultured in Bengal, and belonged to that sect of reformed Hindus known as the Brahmo Samaj. Bhuban Mohan was a solicitor by profession and an amateur journalist and writer of songs. It is possible to argue that Chitta Ranjan's journalistic and poetic leanings were inherited from his father.

Chitta Ranjan was educated at the London Missionary Society's School at Calcutta, whence he matriculated at the Calcutta University in 1886. He then joined the Presidency College, and took the Bachelor's degree in 1890. Shortly after he came to England to study law and to compete for the Indian Civil Service. He joined the Middle Temple, and was called to the Bar in 1892. In the previous year he had taken the Civil Service examination, but had failed to secure a place in the list of successful candidates. During his stay in England he made several political speeches, notably in support of the parliamentary candidature of Dadabhoy Naoroji, the first Indian to be elected to the House of Commons.

Returning to India in 1893, he commenced practice as a barrister in the High Court of Calcutta, but for many years had little success. He also went through a period of acute financial trouble. Bhuban Mohan, who was then in declining health, had contracted several

debts on his own account and, what was worse, stood security for a friend of his for a very large sum of money. The friend not being able to redeem the security, both Bhuban Mohan and Chitta Ranjan—who had assumed joint responsibility with his father—were financially ruined and had to seek the relief of the insolvency court in 1906. It should be said, however, that as soon as his circumstances permitted it, Chitta Ranjan took the unusual procedure of applying for the annulment of the insolvency order and paid back the entire amount of his and his father's debts. The debts had become time-barred, but Chitta Ranjan considered himself under the moral obligation to pay them. This act of honesty, which has very few parallels in any country, is one of the many instances of the magnanimity and large-heartedness that he always showed in all matters connected with money. It made a great impression and was applauded all over the country.

Between 1893 and 1906 the chief events of his life were his marriage, in 1897, to Basanti Devi, and the publication of the first two volumes of his poems, the *Malancha* and the *Mala*. The opportunity should be taken here to mention his work as a poet and a journalist, since no account of his life will be complete otherwise, and for the special reason that his reputation as a political leader and lawyer has somewhat eclipsed the reputation he deserves to have as a poet. Chitta Ranjan never regarded poetry as his calling, but there can be no doubt that some of his poems will find an abiding place in Bengali literature. He does not possess very great originality and does not introduce many strikingly novel themes or forms of expression. Nor does he evince, except in rare moments, the magical power of creation. But the bulk of his work is highly cultured, distinctive, competent, and impregnated with deep thought and feeling. Though very few of his poems touch the highest water-mark of genius, there are very few poets in Bengal, leaving out Tagore, whose average performance sustains such a high level as Chitta Ranjan's. This is because of the high seriousness of his purpose and the abundant vitality of his mind and senses. His themes are almost always profound—questionings on God and on the meaning of life, love and death—but they never remain abstract, and are rendered poetic by the intensity of his emotional fervour and the acuteness of his sense-perception. His poems possess the additional interest of a highly illuminating spiritual documentary. They describe the process by which he gradually cast off the puritanism and the sectarian outlook of the Brahmo Samaj, and the intellectualism, atheism and hedonism that he had imbibed with Western education, and found ultimate rest and happiness in the Vaishnava ideal of love. As Vaishnavism is the finest and the most characteristic flowering of the Hindu spirit in Bengal, Chitta Ranjan's spiritual pilgrimage may be described as his travelling away from the West to the ideals of his native land, and from the sect into which he was born to the larger life of the entire Bengali people whose political leader he was. The note of intellectual revolt, which in such early works as the *Malancha* had led him to the rejection of God, gradually subsides, and gives place, in such later works as the *Kishore Kishori* and the *Antaryyami*, to that ecstatic love of the Vaishnava which is at once carnal and

spiritual, and realises, through its own intensity of pleasure and pain, the infinite and the immortal in the finite and the mortal. In his concluding years he wrote some devotional songs after the manner of the Vaishnava poets of Bengal. His conversion to Vaishnavism was not only the fulfilment of a religious need, it was also intimately connected with his political nationalism. For he stood for a synthesis which would unite the political nationalism of a country with its cultural and spiritual heritage in a harmonious whole. He held that the spirit of nationalism in Bengal should not, and could not, thrive in isolation, as if it were entirely a matter of politics and economics; but must be deeply interwoven with, and draw nourishment from, the cultural and spiritual heritage of that country. His most remarkable poems, inasmuch as they are the most original and have the greatest claim to permanence, are to be found in the collection known as *Sagar Sangit* (translated into English as *Songs of the Sea* by the author and Aurobindo Ghose). The poet's soul and the sea are found there as mutual counterparts, and bound to each other, in their manifold aspects of tranquillity and disturbance, by a bond that is basal and preordained.

Unhoped for, wondrous one, ever elusive,
Wait awhile that I weave thee in my song.
The calm sea lapped in dreams
Trembles to-day in the pale light of the moon!
If it be that thou hast truly come,
Then, O smiling mystery! dwell in my heart,
What time I weave thee into song!
Stay yet awhile,
And with the melodies of the sea and the free soundless rhythm of my heart

*I will thee enrhythm in manner yet
    passing beyond all rhythm!
Bound then thou wilt be in the enduring
    solitudes of my heart!
Wilt thou there not abide,
O thou with the circling robe of dream,
Held fast in that music and stay in thy
    fulfilment,
Eternal, unmoving?*

Chitta Ranjan kept himself in touch with all the important literary movements and organisations of the country, and presided over the Literary Conference of Bengal in 1915. His presidential address was on Bengali lyric poetry. He gave much time and attention to journalism at many periods of his life, and was one of the founders, and a member of the editorial board, of the *Bande Mataram*, an English daily started in 1906. His most important journalistic activities were the founding and editing of the *Forward* and the *Narayana*. The former, a daily paper in English, was the official organ of the Swaraj party of Bengal, and had a brilliant and stormy career for many years. The *Narayana*, a monthly in Bengali, was chiefly devoted to Vaishnavism and literature.

As lawyer Chitta Ranjan first came into prominence in 1908 as counsel for defence in the trial of Aurobindo Ghose, the editor of the *Bande Mataram*. The partition of Bengal in 1905 had let loose a tremendous wave of nationalist agitation and revolutionary activity, and the Government resorted to unusual measures. The *Bande Mataram* was the foremost nationalist paper of the day, and Aurobindo Ghose was tried on the charge of sedition before the Chief Presidency Magistrate of Calcutta. Chitta Ranjan's brilliant advocacy at once brought him into the limelight, but a still greater opportunity came to him the same year. This was the Manick-

tolla Bomb Case, one of the most sensational political trials in history. Following a bomb outrage in Muzaffer-pur, the police unearthed a bomb factory in Manicktolla, a suburb of Calcutta. Thirty-six young Bengalis were put on trial for conspiring and waging war against the King and for acquiring arms for that purpose. Aurobindo Ghose, whose brother was one of the leaders of the terrorist organisation, was put on trial too. The case lasted for a long time, more than two hundred witnesses were examined, four thousand documents filed, and there were so many as five hundred exhibits—bombs, revolvers, detonators, ammunition, etc. Chitta Ranjan, who conducted the defence for practically no remuneration, covered himself with fame by his brilliant forensic skill and power of cross-examination. He also endeared himself to the heart of nationalist Bengal, which regarded the accused as great, though misguided, patriots. This case was the starting point of his tremendous success in his profession. His practice was perhaps the largest and the most lucrative ever enjoyed by any lawyer in India, and his earnings sometimes verged on the record figure of £50,000 per year. His success was chiefly made in criminal cases—the most sensational of which, in addition to the aforementioned, were the Dacca Conspiracy Case and the Munitions Board Case—but he showed great ability in many civil suits as well. The most notable of these was the Dumraon Raj Adoption Case.

Chitta Ranjan had been associated with the new nationalist movement that began with the partition of Bengal, and with its two organs, the *New India* and the *Bande Mataram*. He had also joined the Indian National Congress as a delegate in 1906. But he took no active part in politics until 1917, when he was invited to preside over the Bengal Provincial Conference

of the Congress in Calcutta. His connection with politics which began in this
way continued uninterrupted until his
death. His presidential address before
the Bengal Provincial Conference was
more in the nature of a sentimental
rhapsody than a considered political
speech. He painted a highly romantic
picture of Bengal's golden past, and
attributed the present suffering of the
people to their fall from the spiritual
ideals of ancient India and to their
adoption of the materialist values of the
West. He suggested as remedies village
reconstruction, return to the soil and the
renouncing of industrialism. But his
practical sagacity and political acumen
asserted themselves in the evidence he
gave, in the same year, before the
Montagu-Chelmsford Reforms Commission, which was then touring India
with the object of ascertaining what
measure of self-government should be
introduced in the proposed reforms
scheme. In his evidence Chitta Ranjan
demanded popular control of finance as
well as of all the services, but left the
army, the navy and the railways as
reserved subjects for the time being.
In the same year he played an important
part in the controversy that arose in the
Congress Working Committee over the
election of Mrs. Annie Besant as the
president of the Calcutta Session of the
Congress. Chitta Ranjan threw in his
weight with the left wing, and the schism
that thus began in the Congress ultimately
resulted in the formation of a new party
in India—the Moderate, or as it was later
called, the Liberal Party, representing
the older and the conservative section
of Indian political opinion. Before the
Congress met in Calcutta in 1917 Chitta
Ranjan went on a lecturing tour in East
Bengal and addressed large and enthusiastic meetings in every place he visited.
In the Congress session he delivered an
impassioned speech on India's right to

develop her political constitution according to her needs, and independently of
dictation from Whitehall.

In 1918 he succeeded, in the Congress
session at Delhi, in carrying through the
demand for complete and immediate
provincial autonomy against the opposition of the Moderates led by Mrs.
Besant. His other great activity in that
year was directed against the proposed
Defence of India Act (also called
Rowlatt Act). He stirred up a tremendous amount of public opinion
against the Act and condemned it in a big
meeting in the Town Hall of Calcutta.

The Indian situation became more
critical than ever in 1919, the black year of
the Amritsar tragedy and of martial law in
the Punjab. Chitta Ranjan did extremely
able work in the committee set up by the
Congress to inquire into the Punjab
affairs. He met Mahatma Gandhi for
the first time on this committee, and he
supported the Mahatma when the latter
launched *Satyagraha* (passive resistance)
against the Defence of India Act. A
complete *hartal* (public mourning and
cessation of business) was declared and
observed all over India on the 6th of
April, the second Sunday after the Act
had received the Viceroy's assent. In
the Congress session at Amritsar that
year he came out as one of the principal
leaders of that section, called at the time
the Extremist, which considered the
proposed Montagu-Chelmsford reforms
as "wholly inadequate, unsatisfactory,
and disappointing." He also advocated
for the first time the policy of obstructing the Government in order to achieve
home rule for India. "Co-operation,"
he said, "when necessary to advance our
cause, but obstruction when that is
necessary for the advancement of our
cause."

The next year was the most eventful
in the history of Indian politics. At
the special congress session in Calcutta

Mahatma Gandhi presented his five-fold programme of non-co-operation with the Government. Chitta Ranjan, who was a believer in the policy of obstruction from within the legislatures, opposed the Mahatma's resolution, but the Congress adopted it. Three months later, at the session of the Congress at Nagpur, Chitta Ranjan accepted the Mahatma's programme after entering into a pact with him by which each reserved to himself the freedom of future action. Chitta Ranjan's conversion to the policy of non-co-operation was a personal triumph for the Mahatma. In pursuance of its policy the Congress now proclaimed that all candidates for the provincial councils and the central assembly should withdraw from contest, all government servants should give up their posts, lawyers should suspend their practice in the British law courts, and students should leave government-aided schools and colleges. Chitta Ranjan threw himself wholeheartedly into the non-co-operation movement and gave up his immensely lucrative profession as lawyer. Henceforth he renounced all the comfort and luxury that wealth can give and lived the live of a political and spiritual *sannyasi* (ascetic). He was a *bon viveur*, and had almost perfected the art of high living since he achieved success in his profession. But his conversion to the simple life, when it came, was equally complete. A few years later he made over his entire property to the nation for the institution of a medical school, and a hospital for women. The heart of India was deeply moved by these acts of sacrifice, and he was lovingly called *deshabandhu*, the friend of his country. No one in India or elsewhere had a greater right to that title.

From now on his life was one continuous political activity and a succession of triumphs. Students left their schools and colleges by the hundreds at his call,

and lawyers suspended their practice. National schools and colleges sprang up in many places, and Chitta Ranjan founded a national university at Dacca in 1921. The strike of the Assam Bengal railwaymen and the exodus of the coolies from the tea plantations of Assam engaged his attention for some time, but his chief activity in 1921 was the organising and directing of the Congress Volunteer Corps. To accelerate the non-co-operation movement the All-India Congress Committee asked for the recruitment of ten million national volunteers and for the raising of ten million rupees. In Bengal, Chitta Ranjan's appeal was answered by hundreds of young men and women. The picketing of Government offices, law courts, schools and colleges and of shops selling British goods, the sale of *Khaddar* (hand-made Indian cloth), and every other item of the non-co-operation programme were carried out with great efficiency. The volunteer corps swelled rapidly and showed signs of developing into a tremendous mass movement. The Government declared the movement subversive and put a ban on public meetings. Congress retaliated by deciding to disobey the law, and was supported in its decision by the Khilafat Committee. Thus arose a struggle between the Congress and the Government, and thousands of pickets and demonstrators obstructed the police and courted arrest and imprisonment. Chitta Ranjan's wife, son and sister were arrested, and he himself was arrested and sentenced to six months' imprisonment. Meantime he had been elected President of the Congress Session of 1921, but could not preside as he was an under-trial prisoner at the time when the Congress met.

Congress workers having resorted to violence in some parts of India, Mahatma Gandhi called off civil disobedience, and was soon after put into prison. The non-co-operation movement was on the decline when Chitta Ranjan was released in July, 1922, and he gave it the *coup de grace* with his new policy of "non-co-operation from within." According to this policy the Congress should contest the elections to the provincial and central legislatures and enter them with the object of obstructing and wrecking them from within. Chitta Ranjan enunciated his policy when he presided over the Congress Session of 1922, but was unable to carry it. But he gathered round him a sufficient number of followers to form the nucleus of a new party, later called the Swaraj Party, and succeeded in having his policy of council entry accepted by the Congress in 1923.

From now on until his death he was the leading figure in Indian politics. His policy was amply justified in Bengal and some other provinces. In Bengal, in spite of the shortness of time, Chitta Ranjan organised the Swaraj Party with marvellous efficiency and led it to victory as the largest single party in the Bengal Council. He declined to form a ministry, and under his lead the Council refused to vote the ministers' salaries in 1924 and 1925, and smashed the constitution introduced by the Montagu-Chelmsford Reforms. Another triumph of 1924 was the almost complete capture of the Calcutta Corporation by the Swaraj Party in the first election held under the new Calcutta Municipal Act. Chitta Ranjan was elected the first Mayor of Calcutta, and re-elected in 1925. In 1924 he conducted a successful campaign of civil disobedience against the maladministration and corruption prevalent in the Hindu shrine at Tarakeswar in Bengal.

The Swaraj Party was now all-powerful, and Chitta Ranjan the dictator of Bengal, though he never stooped to dictatorial methods. The struggle with the Government began with renewed intensity after the murder of an in-offensive Englishman by a Bengali youth named Gopinath Shah, who had mistaken him for a person of prominence. The Government promulgated an ordinance under which eighty young men—the number subsequently increased to several hundreds—were interned for suspected complicity in revolutionary activity. In 1925 the main provisions of the Ordinance were embodied in the Bengal Criminal Law Amendment Bill. Under Chitta Ranjan's leadership the Bengal Council threw out the Bill, but it was passed by certification by the Governor. Indignation in the country ran high, and the Bengal Provincial Conference of 1924 passed a resolution extolling Shah's patriotism and self-sacrifice, and Chitta Ranjan supported it. In a speech before the Calcutta Corporation, after denouncing the method of violence adopted by the Bengali revolutionaries, he said: "But so far as their enthusiasm for liberty is concerned, I am with them. So far as their love of freedom is concerned, I am with them." His attitude towards the revolutionary movement was widely misunderstood in India and England; but before long he made clear his position. In 1925 he issued two manifestoes strongly denouncing the use of violence as a political weapon: "I am opposed on principle to political assassination and violence in any shape or form. It is absolutely abhorrent to me and to my Party. I consider it an obstacle to our political progress. It is also opposed to our religious feeling." At the same time he appealed to the Government "to cause a searching enquiry to be made into the causes which have brought about the revolutionary movement in India and then to set about applying the proper remedy, so that there may be a radical and permanent cure of the disease. The Government should recognise that, however mistaken the revolutionaries may be, however wrong and futile their methods and however criminal and reprehensible their acts, the guiding principle of their lives is sacrifice for the attainment of political and economic freedom for their country. The moment they feel that at any rate the foundation of our freedom is laid by the Government, I venture to assert that the revolutionary movement will be a thing of the past. I suggest in all humility that there should be a distinct and authoritative declaration by the Government at the earliest opportunity." These utterances were considered by the Government as the first step towards a new era of co-operation, and negotiations took place between Chitta Ranjan and representatives of the Governments of Bengal and India. In the Bengal Provincial Conference in May, 1925, Chitta Ranjan declared his position as one of willingness to negotiate for co-operation on honourable terms. This might have led to a turning point in Indian politics, but his death intervened on the 16th of June.

His body was brought down from Darjeeling to Calcutta by train, and a procession, over two miles long and consisting of nearly three hundred thousand men and women with Mahatma Gandhi at their head, followed his body to the cremation ground.

As a political leader Chitta Ranjan possessed great organising and fighting power, and was one of the cleverest tacticians the world has seen. But the unique quality of his leadership came from his personality, from the personal love and reverence he inspired, and from the complete confidence he enjoyed among both the Hindu and Moslem communities. No other Hindu leader has been trusted by the Indian Moslems as he was. The Hindu-Moslem Pact promulgated by him was inspired by the highest statesmanship and by a generous recognition of the rights of the Moslem community. In his conception of self-government he was ahead of his time and regarded it as freedom and well-being not only for the privileged few, but for the toiling masses of India. In his later years he took increasing interest in working-class movements and presided over two annual conferences of the Indian Trades Union Congress. No words of his have greater significance for the future of India than the following, uttered at the Congress Session at Gaya in 1922: "Many of us believe that the middle class must win Swaraj for the masses. I do not believe in the possibility of any class movement being ever converted into a movement for Swaraj. If to-day the British Parliament grants provincial autonomy in the provinces with responsibility in the central Government, I for one will protest against it, because that will inevitably lead to the concentration of power in the hands of the middle class. I do not believe that the middle class will then part with their power. How will it profit India if, in place of the white bureaucracy that now rules over her, there is substituted an Indian bureaucracy of the middle classes? . . . My ideal of Swaraj will never be satisfied unless the people co-operate with us in its attainment. Any other attempt will inevitably lead to what the European socialists call the 'bourgeois' government. . . . If to-day the whole of Europe is engaged in a battle of freedom, it is because the nations of Europe are gathering their strength to wrest this power from the hands of the middle classes. I desire to avoid the repetition of that chapter of European history."

GOPAL KRISHNA GOKHALE

GOPAL KRISHNA GOKHALE

FOUNDER OF "SERVANTS OF INDIA SOCIETY"
1866–1915

BY CHARLES KINCAID, C.V.O.

GOPAL KRISHNA GOKHALE[1] was born on May 9, in the little village of Katluk in the Chiplun taluka of the Ratnagiri district on the western coast of the Bombay Presidency. He was by caste a Chitpawan Brahman and he spoke his mother-tongue Marathi with the peculiar elegance of his fellow castemen. A strange legend is related of the Chitpawans, which I have told in the History of the Maratha people. It is as follows:[2]

Once Parashu Rama, the Brahman incarnation of the god Vishnu, to avenge the murder of his father Jamadagni by the Kshattriya king Sahasrarjuna, cleared the earth twenty-one times of the Kshattriya caste. Thereafter he was so reeking with blood that no other Brahmans would eat with him. He therefore went to the summit of the Sahyadris and stood gazing at the sea, which then washed the foot of the mountains, and pondering where he could find Brahmans with whom he could dine. As he looked he saw floating on the surface of the water the corpses of fourteen Mlecchas or barbarians. He dragged them ashore, built a great pyre and burnt them to ashes. From the ashes he created fourteen new Brahmans, who had no scruples about eating with their creator. The meal

over, the fourteen Brahmans begged Parashu Rama to give them a land wherein they might live. The hero drew the mighty bow given him by the god Shiva and shot an arrow into the Arabian Sea. He then commanded the ocean to go back within its borders as far as the arrow had fallen. It did so, thus leaving bare the Konkan. This reclaimed land Parashu Rama bestowed on the fourteen Brahmans. They went to dwell there and built themselves a town called Chitpolan or the Town of the Burnt Heart, which in course of time was corrupted into Chiplun. To themselves they gave the name of Chitpawans or Brahmans purified by the Funeral Pyre.

Whatever truth may underlie this romantic tale and whatever the real origin of the Chitpawan community may be, they have produced a greater number of eminent men than any other in India. The talented Peshwas or hereditary prime ministers of the Maratha empire were Chitpawans. So too were Ranade the great High Court judge, Paranjpye the distinguished mathematician, Tilak the famous journalist and politician and Apte the greatest of Indian novelists. So when Gokhale rose to eminence, he was in excellent company.

Gopal Krishna Gokhale was connected with the aristocratic house of Raste and his ancestors had held responsible office under the Peshwas. His father Krishnarao Gokhale was educated at Kolhapur, where he became a school friend of Ranade. Unhappily Krishnarao Gokhale was poor and his poverty

---

[1] I have been greatly indebted, when preparing this slight monograph, to the admirable work of Mr. John S. Hoyland, M.A.

[2] Various authors have inferred from this story that the Chitpawans were originally foreign immigrants from Arabia, Egypt or even Scandinavia. In my view the legend contains no truth whatever. Exactly the same tale is told by the Ben-i-Israel or Indian Jews to explain their presence in the Bombay Presidency.

forced him to give up his studies and accept a small post in the service of the Maratha prince of Kagal, a kinsman of the Maharaja of Kolhapur. Gopal Gokhale's mother was the daughter of Bhaskar Oka, a well-to-do Brahman of the same taluka. She was illiterate, but after the manner of so many Maharashtra ladies, she was strongwilled and deeply religious and she made a faithful wife and a devoted mother. The early years spent by Gopal in the countryside gave to him what so many other Indian politicians lacked, a first-hand knowledge of the Maratha peasant's difficulties.

When Gopal was ten years old he and his elder brother Govind were sent to Kolhapur for their secondary education; but three years later their father died in Kagal and his income died with him. Thus Govind at eighteen had, as his father had done before him, to leave school and give up all hopes of high office. He accepted a small post in the Kolhapur state on fifteen rupees a month. Out of this tiny income he not only supported his mother and sisters, but sent eight rupees a month to Gopal. Unable to complete his own education, he determined that his younger brother should not similarly suffer.

On eight rupees a month Gopal contrived to subsist and learn; but the struggle must have been appalling. He had to reduce his meals to one and cook it himself, and to read his textbooks by the street lamps because he could not pay for oil. Fortunately he had a retentive memory, a facility for mathematics and a fine constitution. In 1881 he matriculated and as an undergraduate went first to the Rajaram college of Kolhapur, thence to the Deccan college in Poona, and finally graduated in the Elphinstone college in Bombay. There he took a second class in mathematics and won a post-graduate scholarship of twenty rupees a month. He was

now independent of his generous brother and accepted an assistant mastership in English at the New English High School in Poona. His salary was only thirty-five rupees monthly; but to a youth trained to live on eight rupees, his salary, added to his scholarship, seemed wealth beyond the dreams of avarice. He sent part of his earnings to his brother towards the liquidation of his debt; at the same time he kept terms as a law student and coached pupils for their public service examination.

Some years previously two distinguished Brahmans, Messrs. Tilak and Agarkar had founded the Deccan Education Society. It controlled a number of schools, but anyone who joined it had to bind himself for twenty years never to ask from the society more than seventy-five rupees a month for his services. This self-denying rule appealed to the young Gopal and he resolved to become a member of the society. The chief obstacle was his brother. Govind had during the best years of his life denied himself not merely luxuries but bare necessities; and he wished in return that Gopal should exploit for the family's benefit his great abilities. Nevertheless the young man stuck to his point and Govind gave way. They were right, for if Gopal never reached affluence, he won immortality.

In 1884 the Deccan Education Society decided to turn the New English school into the Fergusson college and the first classes were opened in 1885. Gokhale was appointed one of the professors of English; but English was only one of the many subjects that his versatile mind enabled him to teach. He had taken his degree in mathematics and he had published an excellent textbook on arithmetic; so he was soon teaching mathematics as well as English. At other times he was required to lecture on history and political economy. In fact, one cannot but think that his seniors exploited somewhat ruthlessly their junior's many-sided ability. Gokhale, however, was no bookworm. As a boy he had been a useful if not an outstanding cricketer and he was an excellent billiards, chess and card player.

While Gokhale was still a master at the New English school he made the acquaintance of his father's old school friend, Mr. Justice Ranade, in a somewhat unusual way. To celebrate some academic function the New English school had invited all the most prominent Poona citizens. The youthful Gokhale was posted at the door with strict instructions to prevent "gate crashing"; he was only to admit would-be entrants who could produce tickets. Suddenly a guest presented himself without a ticket. He had left it at home by mistake, he said. Gokhale jumped to the conclusion that here was the very type of intruder against whom he had been warned. Coldly he told the visitor that there was no admittance without a ticket. Unfortunately the reputed "gate-crasher" was no less a personage than Ranade, the greatest Indian then living. Flabbergasted for the moment, he looked round for an acquaintance who might help him. He found one in Mr. Sathe, who put matters right and introduced Ranade to the conscientious doorkeeper. The great man was far too magnanimous to bear ill-will towards the young obstructionist, and Gokhale became not only Ranade's firm friend but his devoted pupil, and to be a pupil of Ranade was no sinecure. In the following passage Mr. Shahani (Gokhale, p. 59) has described Gokhale's training:

"Under instructions from Mr. Ranade, the disciple set to work with intense application. Many were the dreary hours spent in hunting up materials; many were the nights when sleep was denied the young man, because work

had a stronger claim. Even fever was not admitted as an excuse. 'Fevers would go away if medicine were taken, the exacting master would say, 'but a Wednesday lost could not be reclaimed' (Wednesday being the day when they usually met for their work). . . .''

This was no doubt an excellent training for one gifted with immortal youth, but the strain of it may well have been partly responsible for Gokhale's early death.

For the time being, however, all was well. Ranade honoured Gokhale by making him one of the secretaries of the Sarvajanik Sabha of Poona, then the chief political association in India. Its communications were always acknowledged and answered by the Bombay government. Under the care of Ranade the young secretary wrote drafts for the Sarvajanik Sabha's letters. Thus he had the advantage of writing English and moderate and restrained criticism under the eyes of a master. Unfortunately between 1889 and 1891 the Deccan Education Society passed through stormy times. The two founders Messrs. Tilak and Agarkar quarrelled. Mr. Tilak was a staunch upholder of the old-fashioned Hindu orthodoxy and tried to keep all his pupils free from modern influences. Mr. Agarkar inclined towards the liberal unorthodoxy of Ranade, who had waived his objections to eating and drinking with his English acquaintances. Eventually the differences between the two friends became acute. Mr. Tilak left the Education Society and the Fergusson college and took with him Mr. Namjoshi, to whom had been entrusted the organisation and collection of the college funds. This was a great loss to the staff, for Mr. Tilak was the senior mathematical tutor and Mr. Namjoshi had been very successful in his somewhat ungrateful duties. The all-too-willing Gokhale was directed to take their places, and he became permanent professor of mathematics and bursar as well as professor of English and political economy. Such labours would have overwhelmed the ordinary man; yet Gokhale still made time for weekly articles in the *Sudharak*. In fact the English articles were all by him and the Marathi articles by Mr. Agarkar. For this extra toil Gokhale refused payment, since his journalism, as he explained, was a labour of love for his country.

In 1890 Gokhale first entered politics. When only twenty-three he was called upon to speak at the Congress in support of a resolution to reduce the Salt tax. He did so with great effect, and he continued to inveigh against this impost until its practical abolition in 1906. In the Congress of 1892 he spoke strongly on the Indianisation of the public services and his speech brought him prominently before the public eye; but while Indians outside Maharashtra were coming to regard Gokhale as one of their chief political leaders, he was unhappily becoming more and more without honour in his own land. Gokhale's sympathies were with reformers like Ranade and Agarkar, but accident had put him in an unfortunate position. His first wife was found shortly after their marriage to be suffering from an incurable disease. Pressed thereto by his relatives and with his wife's consent he married a second lady. He thus incurred the wrath of the Hindu reformers who were preaching monogamy. On the other hand his support of the claims of the untouchable castes and, above all, his partaking of refreshments at the headquarters of a Poona mission brought down on his head the resentment of the orthodox party. Mr. Tilak took advantage of Gokhale's difficulties and stirred up the Poona mob against him. This was particularly the case at the Ganpati festivals,

organised by the extremist wing in opposition to the Muharram celebrations. The students vied with each other in composing verses in derision of the moderate group. Unfortunately both "Gopal" and "Gokhale" lent themselves readily to Marathi rhyme, so that in every poem the owner of these names came in for jeers and jibes, always offensive and often obscene. Some years later this literary campaign reached its climax in the appearance of a play called "Kichak Wadh" or "The killing of Kichak" in the principal theatre of Poona. The author was Krishnaji Khadilkar, the chief leader writer on the *Kesari* staff. The play was based on an incident in the Mahabharata. The disguised Pandava brothers and their joint wife Draupadi took refuge in Viratnagar. Unfortunately Draupadi's beauty roused the passion of Kichak, the queen's brother, and he resolved to make her his mistress. She fixed a meeting with him, but sent instead the giant Bhima the second of the five brothers. When Kichak appeared Bhima killed him. In Mr. Khadilkar's play the eldest brother Yudhisht' a preached patience. Bhima was full of a just wrath and advocated violence. The author intended that Yudhishthira should stand for the moderate party and its leader Gokhale; Bhima stood for Tilak and his followers; and Draupadi stood for India. The actors made Yudhishthira utterly contemptible and Bhima admirable. The play proved extraordinarily popular, but one strange circumstance led to its suppression by the Bombay government. Unexpectedly, the public took Kichak to stand for Lord Curzon. The actors played up to the public and every night Kichak's appearance led to a demonstration against the famous viceroy. The suppression of the play followed, but it continued to be read and enjoyed for many years afterwards by Gokhale's political opponents.

In 1896 Gokhale went with Sir Dinshaw Wacha to England to give evidence before the Welby Commission. His chief theme was the growth of Indian expenditure in excess of the growth of Indian revenues. While he was absent in England the bubonic plague attacked western India with fury. The Bombay government, anxious at all costs to check the horrible disease, were led by their doctors into measures that were not tolerable to the orthodox inhabitants of Poona. Great feeling was roused by the inspection of plague-ridden houses by English soldiers, and friends of Gokhale wrote to him exaggerated accounts of the sufferings of the Indian public at the hands of unclean barbarians. The climax was reached when Mr. Rand and Lieutenant Ayerst were shot when driving to Government House at Ganeshkhind by two excited young fanatics. Gokhale, not doubting the accuracy of his correspondents' letters, made wild charges against the Bombay government. An official enquiry was ordered; but when Gokhale, on his return to India, called on his informants to substantiate their statements, they one and all implored him not to reveal their identity. The unfortunate bringer of charges was thus unable to prove them. He had been deceived. The stories told him were either false or greatly distorted and he had unwisely accepted them as true. After grave thought he decided that he was in honour bound to apologise to the Bombay administration. In this decision he was strongly supported by Ranade and under his guidance he sent a full and frank apology to the Governor in Council. This action greatly increased the respect in which he was held by Indian and English officials; but the extremists were furious. Their papers described him as a mean and time-serving poltroon. Their view—to which Tilak cordially subscribed—seems to have been that when one brings an unfounded charge against the administration, one should stick to it at all costs; but Gokhale was too great a gentleman to adopt this course. He bore patiently his enemies' attacks in the sure consciousness that time was on his side. He proved right. The government appointed a commission to go into the question of plague and inoculation, and they nominated Gokhale as a member.

The journeys necessitated by the work of the Plague commission on the top of his journey to England changed considerably Gokhale's outlook. Before his western voyage he had been a Maharashtra Brahman and probably hoped for nothing more than the restoration of the Peshwa's rule; but whereas Tilak, for all his ability, continued to his death to hold this view, Gokhale became more and more an All-Indian and less and less a Chitpawan Brahman in his opinions. Indeed he was all for joining hands with the Moslems, a community against whom the extremists fomented unquenchable hatred.

In 1899 Gokhale was elected to the Bombay Legislative Council by the Municipalities of the Central Division of his Presidency. He soon came to prominent notice by his speeches against the Land Alienation Bill, introduced to restrict the Maratha peasant's power of alienating his lands. Gokhale, who knew the lives of the peasantry well, took the view that the restriction would only reduce the peasant's responsibility and self-respect, and that the best course was to create co-operative credit societies. How far Gokhale was correct it is hard to say. The Land Alienation Bill did produce good results where introduced; at the same time the Bombay government adopted his suggestion and introduced co-operative credit societies all over the Presidency and with marked success.

In 1902 Mr. Gokhale succeeded Mr. (afterwards Sir) Pherozeshah Mehta on the Imperial Legislative Council. Of this body he remained a member until his death some thirteen years later; and it was at Simla and Calcutta that his reputation reached its zenith. It was, however, clear that he could not in his new office continue his work as a professor at the Fergusson college, and after eighteen years of most onerous service he resigned. It was a grave step to take. His experience and reputation as a political leader and orator had given him very great influence over college students and, as he knew, that influence was sound and moderate. Nevertheless there was no alternative. He gave up his post, which had brought him in the small salary of seventy-five rupees a month and took instead the even smaller pension of thirty rupees a month.

When Gokhale joined the Indian Legislative Council, Lord Curzon was viceroy and dominated by his vast energy and ability every department of the administration. So successful had been his financial policy that in spite of disastrous famines he had a handsome surplus at his disposal. He proposed to spend much of this in restoring and beautifying the historic monuments of India. Gokhale's view was that all such surpluses should be returned to the taxpayers by reduced taxation. There was much to be said on both sides. It is true that the peasants, who paid the land revenue, were extremely poor, and nowhere more so than around Gokhale's home. Still the division of the surpluses among the hosts of peasantry would benefit each one very little; whereas the Government of India were trustees of some of the most magnificent structures

in the world. These had been badly neglected and Lord Curzon restored them to their ancient splendour. Any tourist who visits the Taj Mahal, the sites of former Delhis, the mosque of Babur at Panipat, the fort at Agra, etc., etc., will, I think, glorify the great viceroy's name. Gokhale further attacked the salt tax and here he was more successful as I have already said. Salt taxes have always been hateful and in pre-revolutionary France the salt tax (*la gabelle*) was detested. Another of Gokhale's demands was the reduction of military expenditure. The army was, he said, too big and the officers were overpaid; but the army only numbered 280,000 men. It had to police a country more than half the size of Europe as well as guard hundreds of miles of frontier from the incursions of lawless and ferocious barbarians. The officers in the British army were so badly paid that none of them could stay in their regiments without private means. I do not, therefore, think that there was any real justification for this criticism. The fact was that neither Gokhale nor the Indian government understood the situation. The administration was so poor that once when I was on Lord Sandhurst's staff he complained to me that he had just had to refuse the money for whitewashing a traveller's bungalow! Yet the country was not really so poor as that. What was needed was a broader basis of taxation. When Sir Guy Fleetwood Wilson widened the basis of taxation, revenues poured into the treasuries.

In 1905 Gokhale did the greatest thing in his life. He founded the "Servants of India Society." It was created in imitation of the Society of Jesus and was originally an autocracy under Gokhale. It is now controlled by a body of three with a president and a secretary. Its object was to collect together a group of disciples who would voluntarily abandon all ordinary ambitions and pledge themselves to a life of toil and poverty in the cause of their country. It was a great conception and worked admirably so long as Gokhale lived. Afterwards it was affected by the rapid growth of the extreme Congress party.

In 1908 came the Minto-Morley reforms and their initiation was undoubtedly due to the influence that Gokhale, when in England, had acquired over Lord Morley. He also threw himself into the cause of elementary education. Towards that end he introduced in 1911 an Elementary Education Bill; but, as usual, the government had no money and many of the non-official members refused to support it. Another cause that he championed was that of the indentured Indians. These unfortunate persons were lured by crimps to distant colonies and there abominably treated. I am glad to say that I was myself a member of the Legislative Council of the Viceroy, when Sir William Vincent many years later decreed the abolition of the system.

The partition of Bengal and the treatment of Indians in South Africa were other subjects of Gokhale's tireless oratory. It was when he was eloquently defending the cause of South African Indians that he first met Mr. Gandhi, who was working on their behalf in Cape Colony. On the latter's invitation Gokhale went to Africa. Backed as he was by the Indian government he was able to make proposals that first the government of India and then Mr. Smuts accepted; but Gokhale did not live to see this triumph. He had long been suffering from diabetes, and the ever increasing tasks that he assumed as a member of the Public Services commis-

sion, as head of the Servants of India Society, as member of the Legislative Council, as president of the Congress, as representative of the South African Indians, aggravated the disease. On February 19, 1915, the great orator and political leader passed away. His last words spoken in Marathi to his comrades of the Servants of India Society were: "This side of life has been good to me. It is time that I should go and see the other."

The death of Gokhale caused widespread grief among his followers and great regret among his English friends. Although he was politically opposed to the English officials, he always got on with them very well. Lord Kitchener, whose army estimates he tried so hard to reduce, was very fond of him and loved to chaff him. The magnificent Lord Curzon, who hated criticism, forgave it in Gokhale and was so impressed by his abilities, his self-restraint and his eloquence that to show his appreciation of his critic's services, he obtained for him a Companionship of the Indian Empire. Yet it was not only great men such as these who came under the wand of the magician, but all who met him. Once, when I was judge of Poona, I thought it my duty to call on Gokhale; but as it was a purely formal call I did not intend to stay more than five minutes. He received me with such courtesy and his graceful Marathi speech was so delightful to listen to, that thirty-five minutes passed before I left his little house in Bhamburda. The fact was that if he loved his country dearly, he also loved his fellow men and he could not but be charming to all of them. Whatever his faults may have been, and they must have been very few, they will surely be forgiven him for his abounding love of humanity.

THE RIGHT HONOURABLE V. SRINIVASA SASTRI

THE RT. HON. V. SRINIVASA SASTRI

G. K. GOKHALE'S CHOSEN SUCCESSOR

BORN 1869

BY C. F. ANDREWS

THERE is hardly anyone in India whose integrity of moral character is held in higher esteem than that of Srinivasa Sastri. People may differ from him in politics, but his sincerity is never questioned. This fact tells us in a very few words much about the man himself.

G. K. Gokhale had a true insight when he saw the latent powers of Sastri and thought of him as a possible successor. For there is in him a remarkable combination, which Gokhale also possessed, of intellectual honesty and high idealism; a readiness to face adverse facts, a sceptical frame of mind, a refusal to be led by sentiment. Though these two great Indian leaders came from different parts of India, they both met together on a common political platform, accepting, as an axiom, what Gokhale called the "inscrutable providence" whereby, as he affirmed, only in conjunction with Great Britain could India regain her freedom.

Again, in religious matters the sceptical attitude had predominated with both of them rather than the emotional; yet it would be wrong to speak of either as lacking in religious principles. Their high moral austerity has been itself of a religious nature. For Gokhale always had reverence for ideals and Sastri has the same. While in the field of scientific enquiry Gokhale exhibited the stronger mind of the two, Sastri, on the other hand, has revealed greater intuitive genius. He has more of the bent of a philosopher. He represents in India that cultured humanist tradition which can be seen perhaps at its best in

Walter Lippman's writings. It has also its counterpart in Hu Shih in modern China.

Srinivasa Sastri was born on September 24, 1869, and is thus almost exactly the same age as Mahatma Gandhi, whose birthday was October 2 in the same year. A weak constitution has made it often very difficult for him to put forth all his strength without suffering for it afterwards. Yet, with remarkable fortitude, he has been able to exercise his will power in such a manner as to carry through very arduous work. Born in the highest caste of Hindu society, he displayed, as a child, all the traditional ability of the Brahman culture of the South. But his early career, at school and college, although brilliant in scholarship, did not leave behind it any immediate token of the world reputation which was to come to him almost unbidden in his later career.

After his University course was over Sastri worked his way steadily forward in the sphere of education which he had taken up as his own life profession. At last he was appointed to the Headmastership of one of the celebrated high schools in the South of India. It would almost have seemed that his career had then reached its own fulfilment. But G. K. Gokhale discovered his hidden genius and called him to higher service.

Gokhale had just reached the pinnacle of his political fame by his opposition to the redoubtable Lord Curzon. Both in finance and University administration he challenged Lord Curzon's figures, and was proved to be an even greater master of his subject than the brilliant

Viceroy himself. The latter was large-hearted enough to admire his doughty opponent, and Gokhale's fame was henceforth in the ascendant. When Lord Minto came out to rule in Lord Curzon's place and John Morley was at the India Office, Gokhale in many notable ways became the power behind the throne.

Then, at the height of his career, the deplorable fact was brought home to him that owing to an incurable disease his days on earth were numbered. Nothing daunted he put up a gallant fight right on to the end. Yet all the while, as his strength declined, he was aware that he must act soon or not at all. So he threw his moral and spiritual energy into the work of founding a society, which was to be named after him and carry on his ideas. Ever since 1905, this thought of a new foundation had been much in his mind. He called it "The Servants of India Society." All the last efforts of his brief life which could be spared from direct political activity were devoted to the organisation and endowment of his new Order.

The members of Gokhale's Society were to undertake, after a full probation, a life service. They were to dedicate themselves to the attainment of Swaraj for India as an "equal partner within the British Commonwealth." This last clause revealed the essential moderation of Gokhale's mind. It also made his Society accept the middle position in Indian politics. From the outset, it began to attract most of all men with that outlook.

It is commonly reported that after Mr. Gokhale's visit to South Africa in 1912, where he had been far-sighted enough to recognise at once the original genius of Mr. Gandhi, his mind began to waver as to the final selection of his successor in the Servants of India Society.

There was a time—so we are told—when a single word from Gokhale himself might have persuaded Mahatma Gandhi to join the Society as a life member. But that word was never spoken. For it became evident that Gandhi's gifts were of a different order. It is true that he had already taken Gokhale as his political Guru. His devotion to him was profound. Furthermore, his own readiness to sacrifice himself was quite unbounded. He was willing not only to join the Servants of India Society, but to serve it in the humblest capacity. But for him to have taken that course would have brought injury to his deepest convictions; and every year spent in India revealed clearly that his work had an individuality of its own which demanded absolute freedom for its development.

On the other hand, Sastri's genius was, in a very remarkable way (as I have shown) akin to that of Gokhale. Both of them had dedicated the earlier part of their lives to the teaching profession; both of them had very scholarly minds, with a desire for accuracy in the smallest details that was almost fastidious in its sensitiveness; both were moderate in their political opinions.

Though Gokhale died too soon to make the final choice of his own successor, the members of his Society were able, in close co-operation with Mahatma Gandhi himself, to settle the question by general consent. For, after a very long discussion at which Gandhi was present, the decision was unanimously reached that Sastri should succeed Gokhale as President of the Society, and that Gandhi should be left free to follow his own inner guidance. The years that followed have amply proved the wisdom of that long-considered verdict.

It has been necessary to dwell thus upon the Servants of India Society because it was this that brought Srinivasa Sastri out of his comparative obscurity, and gave him at once an All-India standing as G. K. Gokhale's successor.

The Government of India recognised the importance of the step that had been taken by the Society in electing Sastri as their new President, and almost from the very first the Viceroy, Lord Hardinge, took him into his confidence.

These were the crucial years of the World War, when every help was needed from men of the highest character who could represent Indian opinion. In less difficult times it is quite possible that Srinivasa Sastri with his innate modesty would have remained in retirement at Poona, absorbed in research work and chiefly occupied in his own fruitful studies. But the War made such a leisured life impossible for him, and Sastri himself discovered in the Council Chamber his own powers of oratory and also the rapidity of his mind in public debate. He came to Delhi with Gokhale's reputation behind him, and he was able amply to fulfil the part which his leader had marked out for him.

One of the most dramatic speeches that Sastri ever made was in opposition to the Rowlatt Act, when he protested with prophetic fervour against the attempt made by the Government to push it through in the teeth of public opinion. It was a strangely disturbed Sastri that spoke that day with such vehemence and fire. For on ordinary occasions he would appeal to the ultimate logic of persuasive

argument; but then he spoke at a white heat. He solemnly declared that if the officials took the fatal step, which they were contemplating, they would surely repent of it afterwards. Those who had known Sastri on ordinary occasions, as he pursued the even tenor of his way, could hardly believe that such volcanic fires lay hidden beneath the surface. Very rarely do those fires break forth, but when an eruption does take place those in authority are foolish if they take no notice of them.

It speaks well for the Viceroy at Delhi that Sastri's denunciation of the Government policy was taken in good part. Its honesty was transparent, and

MR. SASTRI AT HOME

An informal portrait of Mr. Gokhale's successor taken with his wife at their home in Madras.

when the Government of India at a later date required a representative at the Imperial Conference in London he was chosen.

Sastri's work in London brought with it his first introduction to the problem of Indians abroad, which was destined to occupy the most fruitful years of his later life and to win him the well-deserved title of India's first ambassador in foreign parts.

At this Imperial Conference, in 1921, he came into conflict with General Smuts, the Prime Minister of South Africa. A great amount of heat was engendered; for Sastri's position in demanding equal citizenship for Indians domiciled in the dominions was quite unassailable; and General Smuts's argument, that for economic reasons this could not be granted, rang hollow. Everyone present knew perfectly well that the "colour bar" lay behind it.

That struggle for equal Indian citizenship was now to form the chief subject of Srinivasa Sastri's political career. His tour round the world, visiting all the dominions (except South Africa, which refused to accept him on that occasion) had this end in view. He was present also, while on the same tour, as India's representative at the Washington Conference in the United States. Secretary Stephen Porter described to me, when I was at Washington in 1930, the deep impression which Mr. Sastri had made on the delegates on that occasion.

In later years I had the opportunity of going round from one dominion to another, and it was a very great pleasure to me to find how much his visit had been appreciated. His noble bearing, his complete impartiality, and his wonderful eloquence had struck everyone. He did more than any other Indian statesman to raise the name of his country in those dominions.

In the same way the poet, Rabindranath Tagore, achieved a similar result both in Europe and America, while he delivered his lectures and read his poems. Mahatma Gandhi's world fame, as the hero of Satyagraha, was to come later.

My next recollections of Sastri are those in London, in 1923, where we used to meet each other every day at the time of the "Kenya Conversations." Here again Sastri was India's first ambassador, as he presented to the Colonial Office, on behalf of the Government of India, the case for full citizenship and racial equality.

Lord Delamere, as Sastri's opponent, exercised great influence in London society. He had been the joint author of a sweeping attack on Indian moral character in a Government Economic Report, which the British parliament had afterwards publicly to disown. His rooted dislike of Indians as settlers was notorious. Sastri had thus to meet both an influential opponent and a very highly organised campaign, whose aim was to stop all Indian immigration into East Africa. "Durban has closed the back door into Africa," the European statement ran, "and Mombasa must close the front door."

Along with this proposed restriction of Indian immigration went the reservation of the Kenya Highlands for Europeans. These two demands, together with the refusal to accept a common electoral roll under any conditions, displayed in flagrant manner a racialism which drove Sastri almost to desperation. He felt that the British constitution itself, on which he had pinned his faith, was being torn in pieces in order to appease a small number of settlers who had become infected with this racial virus. "If Kenya is lost," he cabled to India, "all is lost." This word of his became proverbial.

During those days of storm and stress Sastri himself was attacked by a very serious illness. He was forced to go into a nursing home in the centre of London, where the doctors ordered absolute rest; for heart disease had been the cause of all the trouble and his life itself was in danger. But nothing on earth would keep him at that time from fulfilling his duty to his country. Everything he held dear in life was at stake and he could not lie resting in a nursing home with any peace of mind. So he insisted on speaking at a great public meeting in the Queen's Hall; but this only brought on further illness. The whole period for him was a time of agonising struggle to maintain the Indian cause in an atmosphere where everything seemed to be directed in high quarters against it. His bitterness increased day by day along with his heart trouble. In the end he went back to India a physical wreck and it was a year before he recovered.

When the White Paper was published it was found that on two out of the three main issues—the franchise and the reservation of the Highlands—the Indian cause was defeated. Only on one point was there a decision in India's favour, namely, on that of immigration into East Africa; for it was finally decided by the Colonial Office that no restriction on Indians, bearing a racial character, would be imposed by law. Free entry into Kenya would be continued and this meant free entry into Uganda. Since Tanganyika was mandated territory, that door into Africa remained open also. Yet this freedom of entry, though important, was scant comfort when racial discrimination had been practically accepted by the White Paper in other directions.

On account of his great services to the British Commonwealth Srinivasa Sastri was now made a Privy Councillor and entitled to be called the Right Honourable. But this could in no way compensate for the patent fact, that in a British Colony like Kenya, under the direct control of the British parliament, his own fellow-countrymen were treated as inferior in status and a colour bar had been established. The noble record of British statesmanship for racial equality, going back over nearly a hundred years, had thus been broken in order to favour a very tiny body of white people. These British settlers had the vast unoccupied areas of the dominions open to them, from which Indians were practically excluded. The injustice of such favouritism is obvious and matters have been made still worse by a recent order in Council which has ratified this reservation of the Highlands.

The shock that Srinivasa Sastri then received changed the whole course of his life in the years that followed. It made him ready to respond at once to the appeal to go out to South Africa when the time came; and here, undoubtedly, he won the greatest success of his long career on behalf of Indians abroad.

The story of Sastri in South Africa can be told from personal recollections, for I was with him during a considerable part of the time. He hesitated much at first. He could not forget that at the Imperial Conference of 1921 General Smuts had been his strong opponent, and also that it had been intimated to the Government of India that a visit from him during his tour to the different dominions would not be welcome. He felt, therefore, that the deputation would lose rather than gain by his own presence on it.

In this Sastri was mistaken; and I tried hard to reassure him. When he reached South Africa he found out at once that his fears had been without foundation, for not only did General

Smuts receive him in a friendly manner, as though the past had all been forgotten, but Sastri also proved himself to be by far the most popular speaker on the deputation when any public speaking was required.

Soon after the first Cape Town conference Sastri was nominated, with universal consent, to be the first Agent-General to South Africa. Mahatma Gandhi himself expressed the voice of the nation by suggesting his name to the Viceroy as the most acceptable person to fill that office. Again he shrank back from it—this time chiefly on the ground of ill health. But he was prevailed upon to go out and try what he could do.

During the interval between the Round Table and his arrival as Agent-General I had remained on in Natal at his special request and, when he at last reached Durban, he induced me to remain with him still longer. It was then that I came to know the deeper sides of his character, and also how sensitive he was to the criticisms which were being continually levelled against him because of his "moderation."

While the altitude of the Transvaal tried his heart and was therefore bad for him, when he got to Cape Town, on the sea-level, and also to Durban, the climate suited him, and he was able to recover his strength. His popularity was so great that crowds flocked to hear him wherever he spoke in public. He was able to achieve, in a short time, what it would have taken anyone else years to accomplish.

At Pretoria, I remember, when he spoke at a public meeting in the Town Hall, how the whole of one portion of the large auditorium was taken up by the older boys from Pretoria High School. On the morning after the meeting the headmaster gave a lesson to his class on what he considered to be the best way of speaking English correctly—taking his examples from Sastri's lecture.

At Johannesburg the Dean of the cathedral invited him to deliver a lecture on India and took the chair himself, pointing out the iniquity of the colour bar and its utterly un-Christian character. He became Sastri's close personal friend.

These were only some of Sastri's triumphs. Among his own Tamil people in Durban, who formed the bulk of the domiciled Indians, he was entirely at home. They loved him with an intense affection, and when he started a movement to build a college for Indian students in their city, the Indian subscriptions mounted up to £20,000 and the college was called Sastri College in his honour.

The conference in London with regard to the new Indian constitution saw him there, as a delegate, both at its first and second session. By some strange act of official negligence his name was left out of the final Indian Committee which was to sit in a consultative capacity along with the Joint Parliamentary Committee while it hammered out the proposed reforms. It was semi-officially announced in the newspapers that Sastri's name was left out because of his ill health; but I knew for certain that he had been saving up all his strength in order to be there on that last occasion when the details were being determined. I went to the India Office and made known what I had been personally told about Sastri's keen desire to be present; but the matter had been already decided. Since on certain main issues the advice of the leading Indian members was rejected, it may perhaps have been well that he did not undertake that winter journey to London all to no purpose.

When I met Sastri, on my return from South Africa some years later, he was

ROUND TABLE CONFERENCE

The scene at the first Plenary Session of the India Round Table Conference at St. James'
Palace, London, 1930.

staying at Poona, living on milk and lettuce, and spending much of his time in meditation. I said to him, with a laugh, that he seemed determined to die as a *Sannyasi!* He was extremely pleased with the idea and answered: "Do you know, that was just what an astrologer foretold about me when I was quite young!"

Though he has not yet reached this *Sannyasi* stage of retirement, his travel-ling days are nearly over. Everyone was highly delighted and gratified when he accepted the office of Vice-Chan-cellor at Annamalai University in his own province. The duties are by no means overwhelming, and he is able to live the life of meditation and study that he has always yearned after.

May he thus go on to a ripe old age both for the benefit of India, his Mother-land, and also for the good of the world!

SIR PHEROZESHAH MEHTA

SIR PHEROZESHAH MEHTA

A VETERAN INDIAN LEADER

1845-1915

BY NAOROJI DUMASIA

THE character and genius of Pherozeshah Mehta, the brilliant Parsi
who declared that he was an
Indian first and Parsi afterwards, occupy
a remarkable and in some respects a
unique place in the gallery of great
Indians whose careers adorned the
closing years of the last century and the
beginning of the present one. That
sudden flowering of nationalist genius
has drawn the wonder and comment of
innumerable observers. Undoubtedly,
it was a phenomenon which owed its
birth to the working of the freedom-
breathing spirit of English literature,
deeply imbued as it is with the ideals of
liberty, democracy, and the rights of
man, upon the natural genius of a
people whose intellect is bred to a high
degree of sensitivity by an ancient heritage
of culture. The advent of English
education in this country, effected by
Macaulay's historic Minute, may be said,
indeed, to have planted the first germ of
nationalist aspiration in the Indian soul
and to have begun the ferment of
development which to-day is shaping
slowly but inevitably into the birth
of a new Indian nation.

Among the first fruits of that quicken-
ing was a galaxy of patriotic stalwarts
whose names are familiar to every
Indian—Dadabhai Naoroji, Pherozeshah
Mehta, Dinsha Wacha, Telang, Budruddin Tyabjee, W. C. Bonnerjee,
Gokhale, Ranade, and later, Surendranath Bannerjea, Bipin Pal and Tilak.
These great souls, each of whom might
have been the man of a century of
nationalist endeavour, together with

such Englishmen as William Wedderburn, Charles Bradlaugh, Sir Henry
Cotton and Alexander Hume, Father of
the Indian National Congress, names
imperishably enshrined in Indian hearts,
first blazed between them the trail of
nationalism in India.

It has been said that after Dadabhai
Naoroji, whom Mehta himself openly
acknowledged as his political guru and
to whom, indeed, he paid glowing
tribute to the end of his days, Pherozeshah was by far the acutest and most far-
seeing political thinker of his time. From
early youth he displayed a rare genius for
leadership which combined bold courage
with amazing capacity for painstaking
study. In his instantaneous grasp of a
situation, swift decision, the unerring
nature of his judgment, the inflexible
resolve, boundless enthusiasm and
energy with which he fearlessly pursued
his decisions, and the almost electric
nature of the personality with which he
swayed his fellows, Pherozeshah displayed from the beginning of his career
to the end of his days powers and
qualities that marked him out a born
leader of men, a national genius who
must have stood out in any country.

To full-bodied conceptions of India's
political future, beyond which the most
ardent apostles of Indian freedom have
not gone to-day, Mehta brought the
leaven of a common sense acutely alive
to practical realities and the conditions
by which Indian political aspirations had
to be governed in his day, as indeed
they still are in our own. It was this
realisation, coupled with characteristic

intolerance of visionary policies and a fiery enthusiasm for first principles and logical endeavour, which made Pheroze-shah Mehta the eminently constructive nation-builder he showed himself to be, and which turned his most fruitful activity into the channel of civic improvement rather than into the wider field of political reform.

Not that he did not have his dreams of Indian liberty and national evolution. His speeches are alive with visions which still provide the goal of Indian patriotism. Indeed such was his far-sighted wisdom in every field of thought connected with the improvement and future of this country that in most matters we are still achieving the signposts he set half a hundred years ago.

It is one of the more remarkable characteristics of this man that in all the days of a career, crowded at first with the struggles of a young lawyer striving to build up a practice in circumstances which practically slammed the doors in the face of Indian legal ambition, then with the showering briefs of a successful lawyer eagerly sought after by a clientele that flocked from all parts of the Presidency, and at the same time with the responsibilities of civic leadership at a time when the foundations of Bombay's municipal government were being laid, he was able to think so clearly that he never made an important pronouncement which he had subsequently to modify or recall, never undertook a policy or action which he had cause seriously to regret or deplore. The perspicacity of his mind betokened logical thought which instinctively rejected the false, with unerring accuracy winnowed the grain from the chaff, and created for him that reputation for being right which was his greatest asset in commanding the following he did and the unquestioning obedience accorded to him by his fellows. He never spoke without careful thought,

and he thought back as well as forward. A thorough appreciation of essentials and realities enabled him to eschew error to a degree that won him in his own lifetime fame of almost legendary quality, and invested him with the halo of an arch guru in the field of civic politics which Time has only burnished.

While his contemporaries devoted themselves to the task of rousing the political consciences of their countrymen and of the people of England to the political needs of this country, Pherozeshah Mehta, who might if he cared have striven far more powerfully in this field, realised that the fundamental essential for the exercise of national freedom is capacity for its exercise. This undoubtedly accounts for the whole-hearted zeal with which he threw himself into the field of municipal administration and devoted his life to the task of reforming, or rather of creating, the civic government of India's "First City."

It is worth noting here that Pherozeshah Mehta never regarded himself as anything other than a son of the soil. The thought that the Parsis might be regarded as foreigners who had no place or voice in shaping or influencing the destiny of the native population never entered his mind. And when on one important occasion some of his friends ventured to express a different opinion Pherozeshah made a historic statement in the name of his community which settled that issue for good and all so far as the Parsis were concerned. In a day when the community, which once led the vanguard of Indian nationalism, laid the foundations of Indian commerce and industry, and built the original structure of India's economic prosperity, has fallen on lean times and is relegated to the position of a minority whose voice is lost in the tumult of India's million-mouthed nationalism, that pronouncement by this great Parsi, who never

THE GATEWAY OF INDIA
The famous archway on the landing quay of Bombay Harbour, erected temporarily for the visit of King George V and Queen Mary in 1911, and later built permanently to commemorate their visit.

10*

paused to doubt whether he was an Indian or not before dedicating his life to the land of his birth, is worth recalling. Here it is:

"To ask the Parsis to isolate themselves and their interests from those of the other natives of this country is to preach something not only equally selfish, but a great deal more short-sighted and unwise. In our case, it would be almost suicidal policy. Its ultimate effect would be only to reduce us to insignificance. We are a power in this Presidency as a small but enlightened and enterprising portion of the natives of this country, and, as such, participate in its greatness. Isolated as Parsis, pure and simple, holding ourselves aloof from the other natives of the country, without common interests, common sympathies, and common co-operation, we might still remain an interesting community, but of no account whatsoever in the great march of events moulding the lofty destinies of this magnificent land."

In his birth and the conditions which surrounded his childhood and early youth Pherozeshah was distinctly fortunate. He was born on August 4, 1845, of a respectable middle class Parsi family. His father was a partner in the firm of P. & C. N. Cama which traded with China and London. Being in fairly affluent circumstances he was able to bring up his family in an atmosphere of comfortable living. Pherozeshah went to school at Ayrton's, a famous institution conducted by an English solicitor of those days, thence to another nursery of Bombay's early builders known as the

CENTRE OF BOMBAY'S MUNICIPAL LIFE

Municipal Buildings in Bombay opened in the year the Bombay Legislative Council sent Sir Pherozeshah as their representative to the Supreme Legislative Council; a recognition of the services he had rendered to the city.

"Branch School" and, passing the Matriculation examination, he joined Elphinstone College, of which Sir Alexander Grant, a famous educationist, was head.

His notice was soon attracted to the tall broad-shouldered Parsi youth who played and studied with equal zest and ability and the liberal-hearted Englishman developed keen interest in Pherozeshah, in whom he seems to have foreseen the makings of the stalwart character and high-souled man he later became. Pherozeshah graduated in 1864, and six months later took his M.A. with honours.

About this time Mr. Rustomjee Jamsetjee Jeejeebhoy, second son of the first Parsi baronet, announced an offer of a lakh and half of rupees "to enable five Indians to proceed to England for the purpose of qualifying themselves for practice at the Bar in India." By the good offices of Sir Alexander, Pherozeshah secured one of the five places. He did not enjoy the benefit of this scholarship for long, however, for six months after he landed in England Mr. Rustomjee's fortune disappeared in the great share mania crash of 1865 in which so many of Bombay's richest men and business houses were utterly ruined:

Pherozeshah spent nearly four years in England. They were profitable years, bringing him into intimate contact in a degree impossible to-day with English life and thought with their highly stimulating influences upon mind and character, and providing opportunities for the formation of friendships with half a dozen other Indians sojourning for similar purposes in England, all of whom rose later to positions of eminence in their country's life. Among these were Jamsetjee Tata, Mun Mohun Ghosh, Budruddin Tyabjee, W. C. Bonnerjee, Hormasjee Wadya and Jamsetjee Cama. Pherozeshah's most inspiring contact of those days, as he himself confessed throughout his life, was with Dadabhai Naoroji, already engaged even then in fighting the battle of India. Naoroji was closely connected with the London Indian Society and the East India Association, and through him Mehta had the advantage of being early trained in the atmosphere of these institutions to expression and development of those patriotic feelings which receive a peculiar stimulus in alien surroundings. It was at the meetings of these bodies that Bonnerjee and Mehta came to know each other better and laid the foundations of a life-long friendship. Among other activities Mehta read a memorable paper before the East India Association on "The Educational System of Bombay." The address was a powerful plea for the extension of higher education in India, urging the establishment of a thoroughly co-ordinated and liberally financed scheme of state education from primary schools to technical colleges and universities. In this the young man displayed sagacious perspicacity and foresighted wisdom, which have been amply vindicated by the bitter experience of more than half a century of unfruitful educational endeavour in this country.

The paper was well received, and won for the young law student a reputation for mature thought and able expression. His contacts increased and with them his mind widened into a happily liberal outlook, singularly free from narrow prejudices. He had been called to the Bar at the Easter term in 1868, and in September of the same year Pherozeshah sailed for India.

In Bombay it was some time before he could establish himself in the profession he had chosen. Legal practice in those days was almost the exclusive preserve of some half-dozen English barristers of formidable reputation and forbidding mien. But there could be no keeping out such a pugnacious spirit as Pherozeshah's, armed as it was with forensic powers bordering on genius and a pertinacity which knew neither defeat nor fear. Pherozeshah literally fought his way into local practice and by display of eminently capable legal ability soon won the respect of those who were inclined at first to obstruct his entry. As the fame of his advocacy spread briefs poured in from all parts of Gujerat and Kathiawar and further afield till, between travelling to mofussil courts and engagements in his home town, Pherozeshah was the busiest and most prosperous lawyer of the day in the entire Presidency. Offers of judgeships and various other legal incumbencies could not tempt him from his resolve to pursue his profession, even when briefs were rare and his income barely sufficient to enable him to make ends meet by judicious management.

His first notable appearance was in a case which has become one of the classic causes célèbres of Bombay legal history, the Parsi Towers of Silence case. His brilliant advocacy in this matter, upon which public attention was concentrated to an unprecedented degree, won him the respect of the hitherto aloof English members of the Bombay Bar and the enthusiastic support of his own wealthy and influential community. The famous Mr. Anstey, with whom Pherozeshah was briefed as junior counsel in the case, remarked of him afterwards that the young man had "all the germs of future eminence in him." The even more sensational Surat Riots case, resulting from the introduction of a new licence tax, clinched his reputation, and after it he had no further need to struggle for forensic success.

His qualities were brought out in more striking degree and his reputation for shrewd judgment and patriotic

AN OLD VIEW OF BOMBAY

When Sir Pherozeshah was a child of eight the first Indian railway was opened at Bombay—the Great Indian Peninsula. Above is the general view of Bombay from Malabar Hill at that time—April, 1853.

FROM MALABAR HILL TO-DAY

Bombay to-day—the second largest Indian city and one of the greatest ports in the world. Much of its splendid development it owes to Sir Pherozeshah.

wisdom established still more firmly by the part he played in the acute controversy aroused about this time by the notorious clause of the East India Bill dealing with the right of Indians to enter the Civil Services. The principle laid down by Sir Stafford Northcote in this Bill was devised to overcome the difficulties experienced by Indians desirous of entering the services as a result of the circumstance that the entrance examinations were held exclusively in England. The clause provided for the introduction of a system of selection in appointing Indian aspirants to the services without their having to undergo the examination in open competition. This obnoxious subterfuge, opening the door, as it did, to favouritism and discrimination, aroused Pherozeshah's strong indignation and he poured it forth with unhesitating vehemence. "In itself," he declared, "it embodies a measure of such pernicious tendency that it will sow fruitful seeds of discord between races among whom they are already by far too abundant." Those who know their India to-day can doubtless testify how that prophecy has been fulfilled.

Further evidence of the fearless independence of his character was provided in 1877 when, at a public meeting of the citizens of Bombay specially convened, a resolution was proposed for the formation of a volunteer corps composed exclusively of Europeans. Indignant at the implied slight, Pherozeshah Mehta moved an amendment pointing out that "it is not advisable to resolve on the formation of a volunteer corps composed exclusively of Europeans in a public meeting of the inhabitants of Bombay." In an admirable speech which aroused the admiration of his fellow countrymen and the indignation of the European community, Pherozeshah declared that it was nothing short of a public outrage and an affront to Indian self-respect to convene a meeting of all the communities of the city merely to place before them a resolution for the formation of a corps from which all except Europeans were expressly excluded.

He had held strong views on the need for military training in this country and was a stout opponent of the Arms Act, in regard to which he expressed himself in a manner so admirable that a relevant passage may be appropriately quoted. The speech was delivered at the fourth session of the Indian National Congress at Allahabad in connection with a keenly debated resolution relating to the Arms Act which had been opposed by Telang himself.

Said Pherozeshah:

"You cannot, and ought not to, emasculate a whole nation. It may be said that the time may come in future when these restrictions will be removed. But remember that when once the Indian people become emasculated, it will be a very long time indeed before you can get them to recover their manliness and their vigour. That is my ground for supporting the proposition; and I say it is a practical ground. Perhaps a good many of you remember the case of James II who, when in his hour of peril, appealed to the Duke of Bedford (whose son had been murdered by the King) for help, to whom the old nobleman replied, 'I had once a son whom I could have sent for your assistance. But I have not got him now.' In the same way, in some hour of need India might have to say something similar to England. I entirely recognise all the reasonable, and, to a certain extent, alarming difficulties which have been raised; but I say that, if you strive to follow a really far-sighted policy, you will realise from the lessons of history that it can never be wise to emasculate a nation."

Promising as were these essays of the Bombay Parsi in the wider field of Indian politics and imperialist policies, Pherozeshah clearly regarded them as providing occasion for forays in which his powerfully patriotic spirit found vent and expression rather than as the venue of his life's work. It is not that he did not aspire in the same degree as the other Indian nationalists of his own day, but rather that he saw the vast gap that lay between aspiration and capacity so far as the mass of the Indian people was concerned, and the colossal work of preparation that had to be done before demands could be put forward for political power or emancipation with the elementary but essential justification of fitness for fruitful exercise of such power and liberty.

Another important consideration which appears to have influenced the course of his life and interests at this stage of his career was the need of a steady income. While not extravagant, Pherozeshah's nature demanded comfortable living and professional activity was in consequence a matter of indispensable necessity. This made it virtually impossible for him, from sheer lack of the necessary leisure, to enter the large field of Indian politics in the only manner in which a man of his genius and character could consider doing that. Thus it came about that his powerful personality was projected into the sphere of municipal government. There his masterful nature and practical inspiration soon expressed themselves in a manner for which the City of Bombay must remain eternally grateful. Beyond question the best work of his life was

G.I.P. TERMINUS

The Great Indian Peninsular Station, Bombay, one of the most up-to-date stations in the world.

done in the Corporation of Bombay, to which his friends and admirers later loved to refer as the "Kingdom of Bombay." Of that "Kingdom" Pherozeshah Mehta, for something like forty years, was unquestioned "King."

Some have compared his municipal career in Bombay to that of Joseph Chamberlain's historic service to the city of Birmingham. A truer estimate would rank it considerably higher, since Pherozeshah may be said to have been the father of Bombay's municipal charter, the founder of its glorious tradition of civic efficiency, and its chief guide and mentor in laying down the principles of its municipal administration. So completely did his personality and views govern Bombay's civic life that his presence came to be regarded as indispensable by his fellow councillors as well as by the public whenever any matter of importance was on the *tapis* for discussion, and it became almost a tradition that decisions should go with the views of Pherozeshah Mehta.

He began his municipal career in the early 'seventies, in circumstances that could hardly be regarded as auspicious, with a spirited defence in the face of an angry population of Mr. Arthur Crawford, who as Municipal Commissioner had laid himself open to the charge of reckless expenditure. In the pursuit of municipal ideals and efficiency, which everybody admired, Mr. Crawford, whose name is commemorated in Bombay's chief municipal market, had not paused to consider the trivial matter of the Corporation's financial capacity. Heavy deficits angered the public, which forgot the amenities it enjoyed and heaped abuse upon the Commissioner.

The incident affords striking illustration of Pherozeshah Mehta's fearless independence and far-seeing intelligence. Amid the yells and hisses of an indignant mob which filled the Framjee Cawasjee Hall, he stood up and defended Mr. Crawford and seizing the opportunity to point a moral, laid down a scheme of municipal reform which was later embodied by an approving Government in more elaborate detail in the Municipal Act of 1872. Thus he became the father of municipal government in Bombay. When sixteen years later the Act of 1888 further amended the municipal constitution of Bombay, it was again his handiwork, and it was rightly regarded by the citizens of Bombay as the Magna Charta of their municipal freedom. To put it briefly, by the Act of 1888 Pherozeshah established the principle of the Bombay Corporation's right to manage its own affairs and it became the superior administrative authority in the City's civic life, "the ultimate tribunal whose decision must be final and binding."

In the midst of all this preoccupation in the comparatively restricted sphere of civic affairs, Pherozeshah yet found time for interest in all India issues. When Lord Lytton's Government proposed a reactionary measure for the control of the Press by censorship on the plea that undesirable influence on public opinion was being exercised as a result of "angry recriminations, exaggerated generalisations, pompous historical allusions, petulant expressions of offended vanity or disappointed hopes," he characterised the measure as offensive in the highest degree, unnecessarily repressive and contrary to all principles of good government. Happily, Lord Lytton's successor, Lord Ripon, was a man of different mould and this fine English gentleman, one of the best Viceroys who ever ruled in India, did all in his power to undo or mitigate the harsh effects of his predecessor's regime. His greatest contribution to Indian progress was the introduction of a scheme of local self-government, a beneficent measure which has rightly earned the country's

CENTRE OF INDIAN COMMERCE
A scene in the busy modern city of Bombay.

lasting gratitude. It won unstinted admiration from Pherozeshah Mehta, who saw in it the first step towards ideals long cherished by him for the political development of India. In grateful recognition Pherozeshah Mehta joined with other Indian leaders in getting up a memorial for extension of Lord Ripon's regime as Viceroy. The petition, however, was ignored.

Two guiding principles inspired Pherozeshah Mehta throughout his long political career; firstly, that British rule was the best possible thing that could have happened to India; and secondly, that it was essential for the better administration of India that Indian affairs should become a party issue in the British Parliament.

In regard to the former he once declared, "If I entertain one political conviction more than another, it is that this country in falling under British rule has fallen into the hands of a nation than which no other is better qualified to govern her well and wisely." In the course of his presidential address at the Calcutta session of the Indian National Congress in 1890 he said again:

"I have no fears but that English statesmanship will ultimately respond to the call. I have unbounded faith in the living and fertilising principles of English culture and English civilisation. It may be that at times the prospect may look dark and gloomy. If the interests of the services are antagonistic to and prevail over the interests of the Indian people, it is still only one side of the shield. All the great forces of English life and society, moral, social, intellectual, political, are, if slowly, yet steadily and irresistibly, declaring themselves for the choice which will make the connection of England and India a blessing to themselves and to the whole world, for countless generations."

"England," he said again, "must raise India to her own level or India will drag her down to hers."

In the year 1885, Pherozeshah Mehta and his friends in Bombay felt the need for a political organisation that could express their thought, and the Bombay Presidency Association was born. He was its first president and remained in that capacity till he died. In the year of its birth the Congress held its first session in Bombay under the presidency of Pherozeshah Mehta's old friend and companion in England, W. C. Bonnerjee.

Of the Congress itself, which had its birth in this City, Pherozeshah Mehta was a member from the very beginning. He presided, as we have seen, over its fifth session in Calcutta and in his address made a striking plea for the expansion of provincial councils on an electoral basis. Fifteen years later, as Chairman of the Reception Committee for the second Bombay session of the Congress under Sir Henry Cotton's presidency, Pherozeshah made a spirited defence of expenditure, amounting to some fifty thousand rupees on the Congress Camp, which had been adversely criticised by a section of Congressmen. In reply to the charge that it was money wasted on a *tamasha* he declared that "there is no purpose more important, no mission more sacred than the one which Congress fulfils in the three short days to which it confines its session," adding that the purpose of that session, "to present our petition of rights, our appeal and our prayer for a policy of wisdom and righteousness, for several of retrograde measures inconsistent with such a policy, and for

the adoption of means steadily ensuring the gradual development of free political progress, broadening slowly down from precedent to precedent" more than justified the expenditure. "If we did nothing more than make this petition and prayer we shall not have spent our monies in vain," he concluded.

In 1886 Lord Reay appointed Pherozeshah a member of the Bombay Legislative Council, a position of which he availed himself to push through Bombay's civic charter, the Municipal Act of 1888. He remained a member of the Provincial Legislature till his death and evinced such practical wisdom seasoned with criticism that was invariably so constructive and reasonable that the Government, his colleagues as well as the public, regarded his services as of the utmost value. Fearless in defence of popular interests and in the expression of his views, a trenchant critic of official policy, he did not hedge his enthusiasm with reservations when he found occasion to praise the administration.

He frequently came into violent conflict with official policy. One of the most memorable of these occasions occurred in connection with the Bombay Land Revenue Bill, which he opposed with all his strength and eloquence. When he found that the Government were resolved to carry the measure through, he created a sensation by walking out of the Chamber. This dramatic, and at that time unprecedented, step raised a furore in the Press, and Pherozeshah defended his action in three brilliant letters which he wrote to *The Times of India*, that journal having led the attack against him.

When in 1892 Provincial Councils were enlarged on the elective basis, Pherozeshah Mehta was the first non-official member in the whole country to be returned—he was unanimously chosen by the Bombay Corporation, which he continued to represent as long as he lived. Brilliant as was his career in every arena of public life, it was no surprise to anybody when in the year 1893 the Bombay Legislative Council exercised its right to send one representative to the Supreme Legislative Council by choosing Pherozeshah Mehta for that post of honourable burden. It was a happy choice. His forensic fame, the brilliant services he had rendered to the City of Bombay, his position of commanding power in its civic affairs, his admirable discourses in the Congress which had won universal recognition as examples of statesmanlike sagacity, his work in the Bombay Council and the great reputation he enjoyed for personal integrity of character and fearless independence, had combined to establish him as an all-India personality, the most commanding figure of his day in the country. His election was hailed as likely to be highly beneficial to the Government as well as to the country. This was in 1893. The following year he was awarded a C.I.E. in the New Year Honours List—a distinction which was hailed even by his critics as a fitting honour well bestowed. One vernacular paper regarded it as "a crumb thrown to the Congress party." Referring to it *The Times of India*, which was one of his stoutest critics, remarked: "Mr. Mehta has of late shown an increasing independence of the reckless rhetoricians who pretend to serve their country by embarrassing and abusing the men who are governing it, and we may be sure he always will be an outspoken as well as an able critic of the Government both here and in the Supreme Council."

RESIDENTIAL QUARTERS

Modern flats and houses on Malabar Hills, Bombay.

In that body Pherozeshah appears to have found the proper *métier* for the expression of his towering genius, and all who remember his career in the Viceregal Council are agreed that he achieved his most brilliant political expression there. His outspoken views and trenchant criticisms did not always find favour with the Government, but they inspired a wholesome respect for popular interests in the mind of a bureaucracy accustomed till then to have its own way without protest or dispute. The officials of that august body were not accustomed to such plain speaking as they got from the honourable member for Bombay; and Pherozeshah was charged with introducing "a new spirit" into the Chamber. His condemnation of the notorious Police Bill, a piece of legislation of a most reprehensibly repressive character, as a piece of legislation than which he could not conceive anything "more empirical, more retrograde, more open to abuse, or more demoralising" delighted his admirers and nationalists generally throughout the country, and aroused in equal proportion the ire of its promoter, Sir Antony MacDonnell. Pherozeshah did introduce a new spirit into the Viceregal Council, a spirit which refused to echo official views, to support dumbly official policies and which actually presumed to criticise and condemn them. Among his most memorable utterances in any legislature were three budget speeches he delivered in the Supreme Legislative Council— the first particularly, which made history with its masterly criticism of the financial policy of the "most distinguished service in the world."

One other field in which he laboured long and fruitfully was the Bombay University Senate. As we have seen, he displayed keen interest in education even as a young man and as his power and influence grew, he spared no endeavour to fight the battle of education in the Bombay Council and in the Imperial Council too. His budget speeches invariably contained demands for more expenditure on education which he declared was India's primary, principal and most urgent necessity.

Though not personally connected in any way with individual enterprise, Pherozeshah Mehta was an ardent advocate of *Swadeshi* long before the movement was born, and in company with some friends, including Telang, started a soap factory. Despite solicitous attention from its originators, however, the enterprise came to an untimely end, Pherozeshah humorously remarking of it afterwards that it was a case of self-sacrifice in a good cause, for they lost every pie they had put into it.

His brilliant services in so many fields of national endeavour naturally earned him the esteem and gratitude of his countrymen, as well as official recognition. Public addresses were voted to him by the citizens of Bombay and Calcutta in 1895, the Bombay Corporation elected him to two successive terms as its President in 1884 and 1885—a distinction which remains unique in the annals of that body—and in 1905, the year of the visit to this country of the Prince of Wales, the Bombay Corporation manifested its gratitude and esteem once again by electing him President for that year too. That year was crowned by the conferment upon him by His Majesty the King Emperor of the title of Knight Commander of the Indian Empire. It was a signal honour, and opinion was unanimous that it was richly deserved by one whose record of public and national service was so uniformly brilliant, whose merit towered in eminence that dominated the whole country.

About this time elements of hostility began to make their first appearance against this great public servant. In

1907 a certain Mr. Harrison resolved with European support to bring about Sir Pherozeshah Mehta's defeat at the municipal elections. At the same time extremists in Congress circles initiated a movement against his moderate counsels and prudent leadership. Mr. Harrison's notorious caucus failed, but left behind it a trail of embittered feelings which lasted many years. The extremists' move resulted in the breaking up of the Congress session held that year at Surat—but failed to shift the organisation's adherence from the policy and principles enunciated by Sir Pherozeshah Mehta, who continued to dominate the counsels of the Congress throughout his lifetime. This outstanding dominance —it came to be said that the fear of Mehta was the beginning of wisdom in the Congress—placed him in a position of peculiar responsibility, particularly in the regime of such a Governor as Lord Sydenham. He had on the one hand to keep his countrymen within the bounds of loyal agitation, and on the other to retain in sufficient degree the confidence of official authority. However, his tremendous personality and a reputation established by years of wise counsel, unquestionable patriotism and proved service, helped him to steer clear of shoals on either side and it is a real tribute to his genius for leadership that not only did the Congress accept his principles after the Surat incident, but that Lord Morley, then Viceroy, was persuaded to adopt a policy of encouragement towards the reconstituted Congress.

It was largely the influence of his views which determined the nature of the now historic Morley-Minto Reforms, and it is worth noting in passing that the changes introduced as a result of that instalment of political enlargement in

WHERE THE PEOPLE OF BOMBAY GATHER
A general view of the bandstand and the car park and traffic island.

India, vindicated fully the wisdom and practical nature of Pherozeshah Mehta's lifelong advocacy of trust in the essential honesty of the British people.

Sir Pherozeshah now tended to abstention from Congress politics and the nationalist movement generally, doubtless because he found widening divergence in its outlook from views which he held very strongly. He continued, however, to express himself with all his old force and eloquence on matters of public import, and among other utterances put forth a strong condemnation of the principle of communal representation introduced by the newly enacted Morley-Minto Reforms.

Two years later, in 1913, he made a notable pronouncement on the treatment of Indians in South Africa, which had induced Mr. Gandhi to start the passive resistance struggle that launched him on his road to mahatmic fame and all-India leadership surpassing any dictatorship in history.

Sir Pherozeshah Mehta always displayed a peculiarly jealous regard for the rights of Indians abroad, far in excess of even Mr. Gandhi's zeal, for it is well known that he did not approve at all of the settlement of the South African dispute with which Mr. Gandhi was satisfied. Sir Pherozeshah roundly declared that there could be no compromise on the principle that Indians must have the open door throughout the Empire, and he maintained that there could be no justification whatever for any part of the British Empire to deny to other parts the right of equal citizenship pertaining by Royal proclamation to all subjects of the Crown.

In 1910 he proceeded on holiday to England and spent several months renewing innumerable old friendships, making new associations, seizing opportunity to meet the official arbiters of Indian affairs and to express, with all his firm brilliance, the Indian points of view on all the issues of the day.

On his return to India he continued to display the same zeal in all matters of public importance, but ill-health curtailed much of his personal activity in these fields. He appeared, however, before the Public Services Commission and gave evidence which that body seems to have valued highly. The appointment of Lord Willingdon as Governor of Bombay now enabled the tried veteran to exercise a wholesome influence in the administration of the Province to the development of which he had contributed so fruitfully. Lord Willingdon made it a practice to consult him on every public matter and appointed him Vice-Chancellor of Bombay University, which in its turn honoured him with the Degree of Doctor of Laws.

One of his last contributions to the life of Bombay was the establishment of an English daily newspaper owned, staffed and managed entirely by Indians —with a view doubtless to providing a wholesome corrective to popular as well as official opinion against the views and influence of the Anglo-Indian organs. *The Bombay Chronicle* thus came to birth in 1913, and on its front page it still acknowledges its debt to the man to whom it owes its origin by stating that it was "Founded by Sir Pherozeshah Mehta in 1913."

The first issue of *The Bombay Chronicle* came out in April, 1913, and the paper made rapid headway under the powerful patronage of Sir Pherozeshah and his friends. Mehta, in particular, took the keenest interest in the journal and even went to the length of personally managing its affairs.

Two years earlier Sir Pherozeshah Mehta had helped to found the Central Bank of India with similar objectives as inspired the founding of *The Bombay Chronicle*, namely, the provision of a

MEMORIAL TO SIR PHEROZESHAH MEHTA
The fine statue of this great civic benefactor by Derwent Wood. It stands in front of the Bombay Municipal Buildings.

purely Indian banking house, financed, staffed, managed and controlled by exclusively Indian interests. These activities, it is hardly necessary to point out, were in keeping with his life-long ideal of *swadeshi*. The Bank's first director was a young Parsi who had already displayed conspicuous ability in European banking houses, Mr. S. N. Pochkhanawala. Under his driving power and ambitious planning the Central Bank prospered rapidly and when two years later a severe financial crisis developed out of wild orgies of speculation and overwhelmed the Credit and Specie Banks, ruining innumerable persons and businesses, the Central Bank was one of the few banking houses to weather that disastrous storm. Its subsequent development under the direction of Mr. Pochkhanawala made banking

history in India and when its able Manager was honoured with a knighthood a few years ago, the Indian financial and commercial world acclaimed the event as richly merited. When Sir Sorabji Pochkhanawala died in 1938, the Central Bank was well established as one of the soundest institutions of the kind found anywhere in the world to-day and one of the foremost in India. Nobody would have been more pleased by this happy fulfilment of a dream than Sir Pherozeshah, who was responsible more than any other individual for its foundation, who watched over its first years with the anxious care of a father for his first-born and who regarded it as the foundation, guarantee and nursery of all his *swadeshi* dreams and ambitions.

Two years later he invited the

EXTENDING THE CITY
The Oval and part of the new town-planning scheme to relieve overcrowding. In the background is Bombay's business centre.

Congress to Bombay and secured the consent of Sir S. P. Sinha, who had not yet been raised to the peerage, to preside over it. Arrangements were well under way for holding the session when on November 5 Sir Pherozeshah Mehta passed away, after having been ill for some time.

A statue erected out of public subscription at a cost of Rs80,000 stands in front of the Municipal building to commemorate the services of this great man to the city and people of Bombay. Lord Hardinge, then Viceroy, paid a singular tribute to him in a telegram to Lord Willingdon:

"I should like," he said, "to associate myself with the people of Bombay who are meeting to-day to express their grief at the loss of Sir Pherozeshah Mehta. He was a great Parsi, a great citizen, a great patriot and a great Indian." A fitting epitaph, indeed!

Those who are interested in the life of this great Indian and would like to study it in fuller detail should read the excellent biography in two volumes written by Sir H. P. Mody.

MOHANDAS KARAMCHAND GANDHI

MOHANDAS KARAMCHAND GANDHI

GREATEST FIGURE IN MODERN INDIA

BORN 1869

BY H. S. L. and M. G. POLAK

PART I. INDIA AND SOUTH AFRICA—PREPARATION

IN every period of man's activity there have appeared significant figures to whom history later points as the leaders of a new age. Such men are dynamic, purposeful, prophetic and dangerous to the established order and habit of their time.

Such a figure is Mohandas Karamchand Gandhi, known to the world as Mahatma Gandhi, born on October 2, 1869, in the small state of Porbandar, Western India, where his grandfather, father, and elder brother were prime ministers. His father later became prime minister of the Kathiawar States of Rajkot (to which Mohandas was taken as a boy of seven) and Vankaner.

Mohandas was the youngest child of a large family. Though well known and influential, it was of humble stock. Unlike many of his distinguished contemporaries, Mohandas Gandhi came not from the first, or Brahman, caste of Hindus, but from the Bania sub-caste of the third, or Vaisya, caste. Nor were the Gandhis in any way noted for scholarship. Kaba Gandhi, the father of Mohandas, "had no education, save that of experience." In his academic education Mohandas never went beyond the matriculation examination of London University. For his mother he had a beautiful and steadfast love. Her gentleness of character, her natural wisdom and her deep religious sense made a profound impression upon him from his earliest years. Probably this love

was one of the deepest emotions of his life and gave him the tenderness that is so much a part of his otherwise Spartan disposition. It was in this background that his early years were spent.

Following the custom of his day and country, he was betrothed when he was seven, and was married at thirteen, to a girl slightly younger. Although still children they shared the same sleeping room, and as soon as the boy was physically capable, consummation of the marriage took place, much to his own horror and disgust in later years. His reactions to that period of his life, with its tormenting unrest, brought a strong antipathy to the expression of sex-life. When the fires of early manhood had died down, he vowed himself to celibacy for self-discipline, a fact that coloured all the after years. He fully believed that his child-wife was his own to mould as he liked, irrespective of what she herself desired. Fortunately she possessed a personality and a will not easily subdued to his pattern, and she has always retained some peculiar quality and an independence of her own.

Being of a Vaishnava family, largely influenced by Jainism, he was strictly vegetarian. Yet, as a youth, he was tempted secretly to eat meat and so break the caste-rules; and this for two reasons. The first was his own delicacy of physique and an intense desire to become a strong, healthy man. The second was his earnest desire for India

GANDHI AS A YOUTH
Mohandas Gandhi as a boy of about seventeen when he first went to England.

it is of the very essence of the Divine in man. Though he saw deceit and falsehood all around him, and knew that it was accepted as the standard of life by people occupying positions of authority and influence, he was never afterwards tempted to yield to it, even when to have done so would have brought advantage and no condemnation.

For healing he always had a great love and some aptitude, and when, at the age of seventeen, his family in conclave suggested his going to England to study law, he begged to be allowed to study medicine instead. This, however, was not permitted; law was chosen for him. But the love of healing remained, and though he could not study in the orthodox schools of medicine, he gratified his desire by studying various forms of Nature-cure treatment and by experimenting with these on his own person and on his friends and relatives. Some of these experiments produced remarkable results, possibly not only

to be a free and forceful nation. He reasoned within himself, after listening to the talk of other young people around him, that Englishmen walked over the land as conquerors; they had power to command others; they were meat-eaters; therefore, if India wished to free herself from the domination of the foreigner, she must cultivate strength; and meat-eating was the first step in this direction.

The taste of flesh was, however, obnoxious, and flesh-eating soon ended. But he had done more than break his caste-rules. For the first and last time he consciously lied.

Gandhi has repeatedly called himself a Truth-seeker and has learned, in the course of his search, that truth is a condition of being, not a quality outside of oneself or a moral acquisition; that

THE YOUNG MAN
A picture of India's future leader taken in his early twenties.

MR. AND MRS. GANDHI

An early photograph taken in their home of Mohandas Gandhi and the wife he married as a child.

due to the treatment, but to his devoted and instinctive nursing.

One such striking case was his cure of two plague patients in South Africa, when twenty others, who were treated by the orthodox methods, died. Another equally remarkable cure was that of his wife, who in middle life developed pernicious anæmia and was given up by the doctors as a hopeless case, unless recourse could be had to meat juices and other special treatment. This being refused, the doctor in attendance left the case, and Gandhi's Nature-cure methods were resorted to. Soon an improvement in the general condition of the patient was noticed, the treatment continued, and she recovered. Before leaving India for his studies abroad his mother persuaded him to take a solemn vow before a Jain monk never to touch wine, women, or meat. This vow he kept religiously despite the many temptations that were thrust upon him.

His first days in England were an agony; he was homesick and unhappy. Everything was strange—the people, the houses, the method of life, the idiom of the language and, worst of all, the food. He felt an intense longing for home and its familiar sights, sounds, and smells. But to have returned straightway, as his misery tempted him

to do, would be an impossible act of cowardice. So he suffered and endured. Frequently starving himself, so as to be sure that he did not betray his vow, he gradually settled down, made some friends, started his studies, and set himself to acquire some of the so-called accomplishments of polite society. He reclothed himself, adopting the dress of the day—even to the extent of investing in a silk hat. Strange how clothes have played a symbolic part in the life of this man! He has never just accepted clothes, but used them as an indication of an inner conviction. In after years, having identified himself with the poor, in whose face he sees God, he has worn the peasant's loin-cloth.

He tried to learn to dance, but had no ear for rhythm and, failing in his attempt, gave it up. He also tried to learn to play the violin, but he was not, and never has been, an artist, except in the art of life itself; and he soon abandoned the bow and strings. He turned his attention to dietetics, always, of course, along vegetarian or fruitarian lines, and became, both in England and later in South Africa, an ardent propagandist.

In studying these early years of Gandhi's life, it becomes easier to understand his later developments. One can see in them all the seeds that later flow-

SOUTH AFRICA, 1906

Mohandas Gandhi as a Sergeant-Major of the Indian Volunteer Stretcher Bearer Corps, organised by him in Natal during the Zulu rebellion.

TRANSVAAL OFFICE

M. K. Gandhi with some of his South African supporters outside his own office in the Transvaal in 1905.

ered into full bloom. His innate love of truth, desire for the freedom of his Motherland, love of simple things and simple people, passion for purity even to austerity, tried courage, and quiet moral strength—all these qualities were struggling within him to find suitable expression in a field of labour big enough to call them into play.

Of his law studies, little need be said. He was a conscientious worker, read the prescribed books, and was duly called to the Bar by the Inner Temple, which later disbarred him because of his conviction in the Indian civil disobedience movement. He never applied for reinstatement. His studies completed, he returned to India. On his arrival at Bombay he was greeted with the tragic news that his mother had been dead some little while. The news

had been kept from him so as not to render him unhappy whilst alone in a strange land. Overwhelmed by grief, for a time he felt that the background of his life had collapsed. To add to his distress, his caste people excommunicated him because of his journeying to a foreign land, and, though he performed the usual ceremonial purification rites, orthodox prejudice kept him outside the caste-fold. This caste denial left no resentment; rather, it taught him how artificial were the barriers of caste, and he came to realise intensely the cruelty of seeking to restrict human fellowship. He gained strength from his tribulations.

After some hesitation and anxiety he commenced practice in the Bombay courts. His first case was a trial, not so much of his knowledge and ability as of his courage. To speak in public had always been an ordeal for him, and now to have to conduct a case, even the placing of the bare facts of it before the Court, was more than he could do. He rose to speak, but became tongue-tied. Baffled, he begged to be relieved of his case and hastened from the Court in shame and anguish, vowing never to appear again until he had learned to master himself and could use his brain and body as the instruments of his will. The family fortunes were too slender to allow him to stand apart and study the art of advocacy; he felt compelled to earn money, and he returned to Rajkot to assist his brother in a small legal business already established. There his wife gave birth to their first living child. Gandhi, however, was not destined for a life set in a normal key, and soon the call came to him to move on.

It is interesting to glance back over the lives of great men and to see how circumstances, apparently insignificant in themselves, take them in hand and compel them to a desired end. They seem almost to be a plaything in the hands of a Player; but the Player knows the end of the game, the plaything only obeys the urge that so often seems blindly to move him forward.

The first great period of Gandhi's adult life, covering the years 1893 to 1914, now opens. A small hurt to self-esteem, a disappointment in Porbandar, the offer of a commission to go to South Africa for a year to represent professionally an Indian firm which had an important case pending in the South African Republic, and the first step was taken upon his path of destiny.

Of South Africa and its problems he knew practically nothing. His political sense had not as yet been developed, and of the position of Indians there he had never thought. His clients were wealthy, and he may have believed that South Africa was a land of sunshine and plenty.

He arrived in Durban in 1893, having no reason to expect other than good and decent treatment. Though he had had a foretaste of racial arrogance in India, it was not until he arrived in South Africa that he felt its full force and understood the grave nature of the colour-bar, that even yet prevails there. It is not, therefore, surprising to find that, having made some study of the disabilities and grievances of his countrymen in Natal and the neighbouring Republic, he was prevailed upon by them (when his professional task was completed to the satisfaction of both parties) to stay in Durban and help them to secure redress and improve their status.

He made it a condition that he should receive no payment for his public work, but asked for his countrymen's support in his legal practice, if they had confidence in his professional ability. Throughout his stay in South Africa, and until he renounced practice in 1908 in order to devote himself entirely to the service of his countrymen there, he enjoyed to the full the confidence of a large *clientèle*, but always he devoted a considerable proportion of his earnings to charity and to the public needs of the Indian community.

Of his professional work he says: "I realised that the true function of a lawyer was to unite parties riven asunder. The lesson was so indelibly burnt into me, that a large part of my time during the twenty years of my practice as a lawyer was occupied in bringing about private compromises of hundreds of cases. I lost nothing thereby—not even money, certainly not my soul."

The Indians had originally been taken from the United Provinces, Bihar and Madras (mostly Hindus), to South Africa in 1860, under indenture, at a time when the Colony of Natal was threatened with bankruptcy through an inadequate supply of native African

MAKING SALT

Salt preparing on Gandhi day at the Chaupatty Shore—a symbolic gesture instigated by the Mahatma.

SPINNING KHADDAR

One of Gandhi's followers spinning the Indian cotton-cloth, whose use he advocated rather than foreign materials.

11

labour. The economic situation had been saved and prosperity had been restored and largely increased through the labours of these indentured Indians, in whose wake and primarily to supply whose needs, upon the insistence of the Government of India, there had followed in due course, at first from Mauritius and later from Bombay, Gujarati merchants and traders (mostly Moslems). All alike were denied citizenship rights and were dubbed contemptuously "coolies" (Gandhi himself being known as "the coolie lawyer") by the white colonists.

In the course of time some of these Indians had entered the South African Republic. At first no difficulties had been raised but, as time passed, trade jealousy, aided by colour prejudice, resulted in "anti-Asiatic" legislation and administrative practice by the Boer Government, involving race-segregation and the denial to Indians of civil rights enjoyed by the white immigrants. The British Government constantly protested to the Boer authorities against their anti-Indian policy. It is conceivable that Gandhi may have, all unconsciously, received his first suggestions regarding the method of civil disobedience when, the Boer Government having refused to issue any more trading licences to Indians, the British Agent at Pretoria recommended them to tender the licence-fees and, if the licences were still refused, to trade without them. Later, when the Government threatened to prosecute for trading without licences, the British Agent warmly approved of the advice given to the traders to pay no bail or fines, but to go to jail.

During this time repeated representations, many of them drafted by Gandhi himself, were made by the Indian community against this oppression, and it is on record that the Indian grievances against the Republican Government were included in the British *casus belli*, Lord Lansdowne declaring at Sheffield, in 1899: "Among the many misdeeds of the South African Republic I do not know that any fills me with more indignation than its treatment of these Indians."

In Natal, where Gandhi had founded and was actively working as the Hon. Secretary of the Natal Indian Congress, the situation was not much better under responsible government. He was largely instrumental in inducing the Colonial Office, under Mr. Joseph Chamberlain, to refuse acceptance of the Asiatics' Exclusion Act, passed by the Natal Legislature, on account of its breach of the Imperial policy against racial legislation; but he and his countrymen could not prevent the virtual disfranchisement of the Indian population (excepting the few already on the voters' roll) on the ground that they did not enjoy the franchise in India.

Soon a strong anti-Indian movement was in full swing in the colony, and he was accordingly deputed to go to India in 1896 to represent the Indian grievances to the Government and people. Partly because of misrepresentations in the Natal press of his activities and partly because of the circulation of a report that the ships bringing him and a number of Indian indentured labourers to South Africa in the following year were carrying large numbers of skilled workers from India to take the place of white workers, an unruly demonstration was made against him on arrival at Durban; he was physically assaulted, and he escaped with difficulty in a policeman's uniform.

When the Boer War began, in 1899, Gandhi, loyal British subject and proud of the British connection, reminded his countrymen that, if they demanded rights, they must also bear responsibilities. The Indian community accordingly offered their services in any capacity, however menial, and at last,

WALKING ON THE SEASHORE

The Mahatma in a light-hearted mood taking his daily exercise. He is accompanied as is usual by a small boy whom he is prodding playfully with his stick.

against great opposition, induced the military authorities to accept an Indian Ambulance Corps, whose principal leader was Gandhi. Though the authorities did not require the Corps to enter the firing-line, it repeatedly did so in the great emergency that arose, and Gandhi records that it carried from the field of Chieveley the body of Lord Roberts' son. The Indian contribution to the campaign was praised by General Buller and widely appreciated, even by former political opponents. Gandhi and the other Indian leaders received medals for their services when the Corps was disbanded.

In 1901 Gandhi, refusing costly gifts from his compatriots, returned to India for reasons of health, with the intention of settling in Bombay. But Fate willed otherwise. When, a few months later, Mr. Chamberlain went out to South Africa to lay down the lines of permanent settlement of the British-Boer controversy, the Natal Indian community called urgently to Gandhi to return in order to help them to make the necessary representations on their behalf for citizenship rights. He responded from a strong sense of duty and led the Indian deputation to Mr. Chamberlain. Shortly afterwards, when the Colonial Secretary went to the Transvaal, Gandhi was summoned there by the Indian settlers, whose representation he drafted and, at their request, he settled in practice in Johannesburg, where he felt that he could be of the maximum service to his compatriots. To their dismay they found that not only was the Boer anti-Indian legislation and administration—against which the British Government before the war had so energetically protested—maintained; it was tightened up and added to under the Crown Colony *régime*.

In order to protect the community against inroads upon their few remaining rights, Gandhi helped to set up the Transvaal British Indian Association, of which he became the Hon. Secretary and the draftsman of its many powerful memorials. The Association had repeatedly drawn attention to the neglect by the Johannesburg Municipality of sanitary conditions in the Indian location, where the majority of the Indians resided. When, therefore, in 1904, plague broke out there, Gandhi refused to allow the major responsibility for the outbreak to be thrust upon his countrymen and demanded that it should be placed where it properly belonged. Closing his office he devoted himself to sanitary work and evacuation and to the nursing of the victims, for which he received the acknowledgment of the medical officer of health.

But the mischief was done. In addition to the generally prevalent anti-Asiatic prejudice, trade-jealousy was aroused once more by the distribution of a large part of the Indian trading population from the burnt-out Johannesburg Location to other towns in the Transvaal, creating the impression of an "Asiatic invasion." Pressure was now brought to bear by the white trading community upon the authorities to protect the Colony from this "invasion," and, in due course, the anti-Indian campaign bore fruit.

Two events of importance at this stage of Gandhi's career occurred. The first was his taking over of the full financial responsibility for the International Printing Press and the weekly newspaper, *Indian Opinion*, to which he had already generously contributed by both purse and pen. The paper became an invaluable propaganda organ for the South African Indian population and for Gandhi's own views on matters affecting it. Towards the end of 1904

he had transferred both the press and the paper to the Phœnix settlement, near Durban, which he had established as the result of his conversion to the Ruskin ideal of the "simple life" after reading "Unto This Last." He had already made deep studies of the Sermon on the Mount and the *Bhagavad Gita*, and had been much influenced by Tolstoy's writings. Here he set up a little colony of Indian and European friends and colleagues who lived and worked happily together in public service. During the later Passive Resistance struggle the paper helped greatly, under Gandhi's guidance and inspiration, to preserve unity among his countrymen, to encourage the Hindu-Mohammedan collaboration for which he has always stood, and to explain to the outside world the motives underlying the struggle and its objective.

In 1906 there occurred the Native Rebellion in Natal. In this new emergency the Indian community, under Gandhi's leadership, offered a stretcher-bearer company to the Government, who accepted it, with Gandhi as its sergeant-major. The company rendered valuable service and upon its disbandment at the end of the rebellion the community received the warm thanks of the Government.

In 1902 the Transvaal Government, upon an assurance to the Indian community that this would be the final identification requirement, had induced the leaders to agree to the exchange of the old Boer residential licence receipts for immigration permits to male Indians bearing the owner's right thumb impression.

Scarcely, however, had Gandhi returned to Johannesburg after the rebellion, than a draft ordinance was published, cancelling, in breach of Lord Milner's earlier undertaking, the permits issued to the Asiatic settlers. It required

men and women alike to
satisfy the authorities afresh
of their *bona fides*, by
making application for
certificates of registration
bearing a full set of finger
impressions, previously demanded only of convicted
prisoners.

A mass meeting of protest
was held in Johannesburg,
which he addressed and
which, at Gandhi's instance,
took an oath to adopt
Passive Resistance and to
go to jail rather than accept
a law that was regarded as
an insult to the Indian
community and to the
Motherland. As a result
of energetic representations
the Indian leaders secured
the exclusion of women
from the proposed legislation, but they failed to
persuade the Government
to drop the measure, which
was ultimately passed by
the Legislative Council.
As the ordinance was of
a differential character,
it was reserved for the royal assent.

With a view to prevent this, Gandhi
and a colleague were sent to England
as a deputation. In consequence of
their activities in London, the South
Africa British Indian Committee was
set up there, with Lord Ampthill as its
president, and in the end the royal
assent was refused.

This result, whilst welcomed as a
great victory for right and justice by
the South African Indian community
and by the public in India, was deeply
resented by the white population of
the Transvaal. Within a few months
responsible Government was accorded
to the Colony, and the first important

THE WOMAN'S SIDE

*Mrs. M. Sanger and the Mahatma discussing problems
connected with Indian women's social welfare.*

measure passed by the new legislature
was the almost textual re-enactment of
the disallowed ordinance. The royal
assent was, notwithstanding the strong
protests of the Indian community and
of the Government of India, given in
view of the new constitutional status of
the Colony, and the historic Passive
Resistance Campaign was immediately
launched by the Indian community under
Gandhi's guidance. Gandhi and a
number of other leaders were arrested,
convicted and imprisoned; but the
campaign continued to gather force,
until the Botha Government decided to
negotiate with Gandhi through General
Smuts, the Minister of the Interior. An

agreement was reached, upon the basis of voluntary registration. According to Gandhi's statement to his compatriots immediately upon his release and uncontradicted at the time by the authorities, when the voluntary registration was successfully completed the "Black Act" (No. 2 of 1907) was to be repealed, and the voluntary registration certificates were to be validated.

A few of his countrymen failed to appreciate the subtle distinction between the voluntary and the compulsory giving of finger impressions and charged him with betrayal of the cause, threatening his life if he attempted to register. Undeterred, he was proceeding to the registration office to be the first to do so when he was set upon by a Pathan and nearly killed. Upon regaining consciousness, however, and before receiving medical attention, he made his application, thus rallying his compatriots.

The dismay of Gandhi and his people, therefore, was great when, at the end of the period fixed for voluntary re-registration, which was duly completed, the Government introduced and passed new legislation validating the voluntary certificates and giving them equal effect to the few that had been issued under the "Black Act," but omitting all provision for repeal of that Act. At a public meeting, held in Johannesburg, the new Act was denounced, the voluntary certificates were consigned to the flames, and Passive Resistance was renewed in July, 1908. Many hundreds of Indians (including Gandhi repeatedly, as well as his wife and other members of his family) suffered imprisonment, and many Indian homes and businesses were broken up. The struggle did not actually cease until June, 1914, when, after many fluctuations of fortune, the "Black Act" was finally repealed, as was the £3 annual tax upon ex-indentured Indians in Natal; Indian marriages, upon whose validity the courts had cast doubt, were legalised for immigration purposes; and the status of the Indian community was, for the time being, at least stabilised.

Three episodes in particular stand out in the campaign. The first was Gandhi's second mission to England, in 1909, upon his return from which he published his confession of faith in a pamphlet entitled "Hind Swaraj" or "Indian Home Rule." A parallel mission carried on propaganda in India, under the guidance of Mr. G. K. Gokhale, gaining support from Government and public alike, and resulting in the stoppage of indentured labour for Natal in 1910 and in a strong protest in 1913, by the Viceroy, Lord Hardinge, against the Indian treatment in South Africa.

The second was the great march into the Transvaal, led by Gandhi, in 1913, of Natal Indian indentured labourers, to court imprisonment as a protest against the failure of the Union Government to carry out its undertaking to Mr. Gokhale, during his visit to South Africa in 1912, to repeal the £3 tax.

The third was Gandhi's refusal, when he was on the point of resuming the struggle because of General Smuts' unwillingness to introduce the necessary remedial legislation, to take advantage of the Government's embarrassment during the general strike of European workers in the Transvaal, early in 1914.

Finally, won over by the passive resisters, by Gandhi's able advocacy of Indian rights, and by the representations of a high official deputed by the Government of India to assist in a settlement, the long drawn-out struggle was brought to an end, and Gandhi, amid the applause and with the goodwill of all sections, of the population, European and Indian, felt at last free to return to the Motherland to begin the public work for which his soul had long thirsted.

ROUND TABLE CONFERENCE, 1931
Mahatma Gandhi leaving St. James' Palace with other Indian Delegates.

DURING THE DISCUSSION
The scene inside St. James' Palace. Lord Sankey is in the chair. Mahatma Gandhi on his left and Pandit Malaviva next to him.

Part II.   The Mahatma

HE went first to England, arriving there on the eve of the outbreak of the Great War. Immediately he set himself to the task of organising among the resident Indian community an Ambulance Corps for service at the Front. But ill health prevented his accompanying it and, upon his recovery, he was obliged to proceed to India, where he arrived, in 1915, just before the death of Gokhale.

Soon after his arrival, and in pursuance of a promise made to Gokhale, Gandhi began a year's tour of his Motherland, after an absence of fourteen years. His overseas work against powerful odds and his great personal sacrifices had already established him firmly in the hearts and imagination of his countrymen, many of whom endowed him with the qualities of a superman, and the title of Mahatma (Great Soul) was conferred upon him by the people.

Gandhi's first work after the tour was to establish near Ahmedabad an Ashram, or retreat, where a little group of men and women settled who had accepted his general principles. Here were tried out the methods of the simple collective life that had been begun in South Africa, without restrictions of class, creed, or caste. Soon a problem arose that tested the fundamental tenets of the settlement—some untouchables sought admission to it. Gandhi consulted his followers and it was agreed that the untouchables should not be refused. As a result, the financial support of the orthodox, upon which the Ashram had greatly depended, was withdrawn, and he found himself without resources. When he realised this, he declared: "We will then have to leave here and live in the untouchable

quarter with them." However, the situation was saved by a timely anonymous gift that enabled him to continue his work.

Meanwhile the agitation against indentured labour emigration to British colonies overseas had been steadily growing and its suspension was demanded. Gandhi, who had in South Africa fought the system, which had been denounced by Sir W. W. Hunter as "semi-slavery," now led the attack upon it once more, as degrading to India. All shades of opinion were united in support of this campaign. Success was reached in 1917, and, shortly after the War, indentured labour emigration was finally prohibited.

People had by now begun to turn instinctively to Gandhi for help and leadership in obtaining redress of grievances. Complaints of the conditions of the indigo-cultivators in Champaran (Bihar) were brought to him. He went into the question, collected the facts, and sought an interview with the planters to discuss the matter; but he received scant sympathy or courtesy from them and, regarding him as a stranger, they requested his non-intervention. Nor were the authorities any more helpful. He proclaimed an open campaign against the methods of indigo cultivation and, disobeying an order to leave the district, was arrested. But his detention was of short duration. In court he gave a closely reasoned statement as to his position in Champaran, and telegraphed an appeal to the Viceroy to intervene, with the result that the proceedings were withdrawn and he was enabled to set up a private inquiry into the Champaran ryots' grievances. Ultimately a committee of inquiry was set up by the

MAHATMA GANDHI WITH MRS. NAIDU

Lieut.-Governor of Bihar, to which he was appointed. It found substantially in favour of the ryots and made important recommendations to which effect was duly given. So began the work that he had long hoped to undertake of agrarian reform and the improvement of village conditions.

A labour dispute in the Ahmedabad mills led to his first public fast. Gandhi had extracted from the strikers a promise to stand firm and to do so without violence of word or deed. Too much, probably, was expected of them; they began to falter, and the strike looked like collapsing. To rally them again he took a tremendous resolution, vowing not to touch food until the strike was settled. He said afterwards that he realised that he had by his action placed an unfair burden upon the mill-owners, many of whom were his friends; for so great a following had Gandhi that

they were compelled to come to terms rather than let ill befall him. Thus the strikers won, if not all they asked for, a considerable part of it, and a new weapon in dealing with public affairs was forged—that of suffering in one's own person for the sins or errors of others. It implied no new doctrine, but as a method of securing redress of a collective wrong it had not been used before. It struck the public imagination. *Satyagraha* (Soul-force) was now to be pitted against physical force: would it prove a mightier power? Much was said and written about it and the method and circumstances of its exercise, and the influence which Gandhi had already gained over the minds and hearts of men grew rapidly.

No sooner was the mill strike over than a new struggle began which put into operation *Satyagraha*. In Kaira district the crops failed, famine conditions threatened, and many cultivators were unable to pay the tax demands. Gandhi was called to their aid. He drafted a petition, and therein exercised the statutory right to ask for suspension of revenue collections; but the petition failed. Then Gandhi advised the sufferers and their sympathisers to refrain from attempting to pay; they should not sell their all and thus permanently impoverish or ruin themselves. "Refuse to pay," he said; "even those of you who can, and take the consequences at the hands of the Law." News of the struggle spread over India; money was sent to help the fight. Time passed, and the peasants began to lose nerve under the threats of the officials and at the sight of their cattle and goods seized and sold. Standing crops in some cases were attached and Gandhi grew anxious as he saw the wavering of the people. Again something urgent had to be done. He therefore suggested to some of his followers that they should remove the crops themselves from a field that had been attached. He knew that this might mean their being arrested, but all were willing to test it out. They were arrested and given short terms of imprisonment. Fortunately the struggle ended soon by an agreed compromise. But the Kaira struggle was a great step in the awakening of the masses of India to a sense of their rights and their own ability to secure redress. They were not to sleep again.

Of Gandhi's passion for unity amongst his countrymen much could be said. By pleading, by argument, by suffering and by example he sought most earnestly and diligently to weld into one strong whole the two main streams of Indian life, Hindu and Moslem. By his work for the Khalifat movement, under the leadership of the Ali brothers, he hoped to bring this desired end nearer, apart from the merits of the movement itself.

It has to be confessed, however, that in this he has not been successful, though many Moslems have enrolled under his banner and that of the Indian-National Congress, and many call him brother.

Killing he has hated in any guise. That it was done as organised warfare could not exalt it in his eyes. But to refrain from the fight through cowardice was to him a greater crime than that of war itself. One did not then refrain from killing out of love, but because of fear for one's own person. So once again, and after much heart-searching, he led a recruiting campaign in the latter part of the Great War, on the ground that the quickest and straightest way to win Swaraj was to help to defend the Empire. Simultaneously, he addressed to the Viceroy an eloquent plea for a fuller understanding of India's national sentiment and a due recognition of her place in the British Commonwealth of Nations.

Under the continued strain that he had put upon himself for so long, his health gave way and he came near to death. His doctors were baffled by his illness and urged him to take milk as being the only food suited to his enfeebled condition. He had, however, for some time observed a vow not to take it, as a food calculated to stimulate the passions. With great subtlety, Mrs. Gandhi prevailed upon him to listen to the doctors by reminding him that his vow was against cow's milk, but not against the milk of the goat. From then dates the Goat as the symbol of Gandhi's abstemiousness in diet.

Soon after his recovery came the Rowlatt Act, against which British India, towns and villages alike, was united. A *hartal* (general cessation of work) at the opening of the struggle was proclaimed and widely observed throughout the country. Thus his work of rousing and uniting India continued.

Young India, a weekly newspaper, became his mouthpiece. His method of work had undergone no radical change from that of South Africa, but his field of action was now enlarged, and when his nation-wide non-co-operation movement was started, the ground had been well prepared.

In 1920, whilst the Khalifat agitation was still in progress, the Punjab disorders occurred, as a result of post-war economic distress and in protest against oppressive administration. When the news became known of the manner in which they had been suppressed by Sir Michael O'Dwyer's Government, culminating in the Jallianwala Bagh shooting at Amritsar, bitter indignation was voiced all over India. An official committee of inquiry was set up, but the Indian National Congress, which had appointed a sub-committee of its own, under Gandhi's chairmanship, refused to collaborate. The sub-committee's report, after meticulous examination of witnesses, was accepted by Indian opinion in preference to the milder one of the official committee. When the matter came up for discussion in the House of Commons, General Dyer's action was condemned; but in the House of Lords, on the contrary, it was vindicated. This unfortunate result was deeply resented in India. Gandhi joined forces with those who, as a protest against what was regarded as British injustice and indifference to Indian sentiment and self-respect, were urging the boycott of the councils set up under the Montagu-Chelmsford reforms. He enunciated four stages in the programme of non-co-operation: (1) to give up titles and honorary offices; (2) to refuse to serve the Government in paid appointments or to participate in any manner in the working of the existing machinery of Government; (3) to decline to pay taxes in support of it; and (4) to ask the police and the military to withdraw co-operation from the Government.

He himself returned his Kaisar-i-Hind medal, and he pursued an energetic campaign in support of his views in *Young India*. At a special session of the Congress his resolution to adopt non-co-operation throughout British India was carried by a large majority, though the minority was substantial and influential. His commanding influence over the Congress was finally established at the ensuing regular session. Had the movement succeeded as he had hoped, it would undoubtedly have gone far to paralyse the Government. But the "plan of campaign" did not work out as he had foreseen. Whilst jail became a familiar place to large numbers who followed him both in precept and in practice, the mass of the people, unprepared for the sacrifice and the self-discipline demanded of them, were unable to carry on the struggle with fortitude and calm. Internal troubles arose, many of the leaders doubted the political wisdom of remaining out of the legislatures, and on various occasions mob-violence occurred. Gandhi was horrified by these evident failures of his passionately-held doctrine of *Ahimsa* (non-violence), and he called off the civil disobedience movement against which, he felt, God had set His face.

He was convinced that the masses were as yet unprepared for a great non-violent struggle for freedom. Moreover, he had begun to realise increasingly that seasonal unemployment and intemperance were playing havoc with the vitality and the economic resources of the people. In addition, they were weakened by social divisions. He accordingly began to devote himself to the preaching of the use of the *charka* (hand-loom) and the spinning and weaving of *khaddar* (cotton-cloth) as a discipline and a primary means of improving village-welfare; the abolition of the liquor-traffic; and the removal of untouchability. He has lately organised a movement for mass-education, so far as possible on a self-supporting basis, by methods combining training of the hand and the mind. But for him education is first a question of character development.

In 1924, the year in which he fasted at Delhi to obtain Hindu-Moslem unity, he was unanimously elected president of the Congress and he enunciated vigorously his economic and social programme. He also spoke fervently of his belief in India's political goal as that of an equal member among the interdependent countries of the Commonwealth.

In place of *Young India*, which disappeared during a later non-co-operation campaign, he brought out the weekly *Harijan*, in order to advocate primarily the abolition of untouchability, but it was also used as his channel of communication regarding his many activities and interests, including his replies to correspondents from all over the world.

By 1929 a new atmosphere of intense emotion had developed with the growing self-consciousness of Nationalist India. There were now three main parties in the country: the Central Government, in whom was vested power, subject to the British Parliament; the Congress, full of spirit, restless energy, intense patriotic feeling and strong racial resentment; and the Moderates, widely experienced, but with little influence over the masses. At the Lahore Congress a notable difference of opinion occurred between Gandhi and Pundit Jawaharlal Nehru, the then president of the Congress and spokesman of Young India. The latter pressed for a declaration of complete independence (Purna Swaraj); the former insisted upon

an interpretation of the term in the sense of Dominion Self-Government. In the end, no hard and fast definition of Swaraj was or has since been made by the Congress, though Gandhi, as late as the beginning of 1937, once more proclaimed his belief in Dominion status for India, as defined by the Statute of Westminster, as a fulfilment of India's political ambitions. He remains of the opinion that she can achieve the substance of independence whilst continuing, as an equal member, within the British Commonwealth of Nations (*Harijan*, June 24, 1939).

Gandhi has always possessed a strange instinct for the use of dramatic gesture and symbolism, often with spectacular results. One such was his decision to start a new non-violent campaign to secure the abolition of the salt-tax, which was held to oppress the very poor. He and some colleagues, early in 1930, accordingly set out for the seashore at Dandi in order to break the law by preparing salt, a Government monopoly, and he was arrested and imprisoned. His example was followed, and soon civil disobedience was prevalent once more throughout the country and repressive measures were adopted by the Government.

Another illustration of his gift for symbolic dramatisation was the public burning of foreign cloth, at his instance, partly to hit the Government's revenues and partly in aid of the *swadeshi* (home industries) movement. The familiar "Gandhi cap," part of the Congress uniform of *khaddar*, is another instance, for it is a replica of the convict's cap worn by him in the Transvaal jail.

It had, however, already been realised, both at Delhi and in London, that the time was ripe for further constitutional advance in India. A Round Table Conference was called in London, but the Congress at first refused to partici-

CROSSING THE FRONTIER
Mahatma Gandhi and a band of followers fording the Swat River.

pate in its deliberations. Lord Irwin, however, took steps soon after Gandhi's release from prison, to invite him to a meeting at Delhi, and shortly afterwards the Gandhi-Irwin Pact was announced (March 3, 1931), civil disobedience being suspended. The Pact was ratified at the Karachi session of the Congress.

Gandhi proceeded to London as its sole representative at the second Round Table Conference. In London, again in symbolic mood, he insisted upon living in a working-class district in order to be among the poor, and upon wearing his *khaddar* loin-cloth and shawl even when he visited King George V at Buckingham Palace. His heart, however, was not in the deliberations of the Conference, to which he made little effective contribution, but where he claimed to represent the impoverished masses and the "depressed classes" of India. He felt restless that

he was adding little to the welfare of his "fellow-villagers" at home. He, however, took repeated occasion to deliver his message of non-violence to the Western world.

Upon his return to India, early in 1932, he found the stage set against all his hopes. Charges of breach of the Pact, under Lord Irwin's successor, had been made by the Congress leaders and several of his closest colleagues had already been arrested or imprisoned before his arrival. He, too, was arrested and imprisoned, in an atmosphere of mutual suspicion, upon his announcing the resumption of civil disobedience.

One of the matters outstanding at the end of the Round Table Conference was the question of the representation of the minority communities. Owing to the inability of the Indian leaders there to agree upon quotas and methods of representation, the Prime Minister issued his Communal Award. Gandhi took deep offence at the segregation of the depressed classes from the rest of the Hindu community, and undertook a "fast unto death" whilst still in jail, until the leaders of the community generally and of the depressed classes reached an agreement, which was subsequently adopted by the British authorities. Much resentment was, however, aroused in Hindu circles, especially in Bengal, at the limited representation left to the general Hindu body of electors after the claims of the depressed classes had been met. Criticism, too, was widespread in more thoughtful circles at the use of the fast by Gandhi in circumstances that bore the appearance of moral coercion, since nobody would willingly become responsible for the Mahatma's death.

After Gandhi's release, some time later, when the civil disobedience movement had collapsed, he continued to devote himself to social and economic reform work. He gradually withdrew from political activities and ultimately resigned his membership of the Congress. But it had learnt to depend upon his advice and guidance, and he has remained its unofficial leader and its referee and arbiter in great emergencies. This was particularly notable at the time when, with his strong support and after a reassuring pronouncement by the Viceroy, the new Indian constitution came into force, early in 1937, by the establishment of autonomy in the British Indian Provinces, in most of which Congress Governments were set up.

A further occasion of the demonstration of his powerful influence was when a change of Premier was brought about in the Congress Government in the Central Provinces after reference to him by the Working Committee of the Congress.

A striking illustration, however, of the

unique position that he holds as the acknowledged leader of the Indian nationalist forces is the fact that, after the re-election of Mr. S. C. Bose as President of the Congress by the Provincial Congress Committees, quite recently, in spite of Gandhi's support of another candidate, the annual session of the Congress that followed almost immediately reiterated its complete confidence in him, resolved to support his policies, and virtually instructed Mr. Bose to appoint a Working Committee that would enjoy Gandhi's confidence. Mr. Bose, however, failed to secure the support of Gandhi's nominees, and resigned the Presidentship, the new President, Dr. Rajendra Prasad, being an old colleague of the Mahatma's and the new Working Committee being composed entirely of his supporters.

The most recent symbolic episode in Gandhi's career was his "fast unto death" early in 1939, at Rajkot. He determined upon this in order to compel the ruler of that small State to abide by what he contended the latter had undertaken in the appointment of the personnel of a committee to make proposals for constitutional reform in the State. He consented to abandon the fast after the dispute had been referred for an opinion to the Federal Chief Justice by the Viceroy, whom Gandhi had requested to intervene as the representative of the Paramount Power. In the result his contention was upheld; but to the general astonishment he subsequently renounced the advantages of the award as having been obtained by the coercion of the ruler and being thus "tainted with *Himsa* (violence)."

Two characteristic expressions of Gandhi's independence of judgment here call for notice. The first is his advice to the Congress leaders, in the face of Mr. Bose's demand to present Britain with an ultimatum in the prevailing international

THE FAST AT RAJKOT

Early in 1939 *Mahatma Gandhi decided to embark on a "fast unto death." He did this as a protest against the ruler of Rajkot who, he insisted, had not carried out certain promises in connection with reforms in the government of his state. The Viceroy intervened, and the matter was referred to the Federal Chief Justice. Gandhi then abandoned his fast. His opinion was subsequently upheld.*

DISCUSSING THE MATTER WITH
A FELLOW TRAVELLER

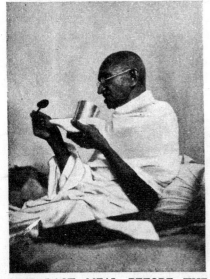

THE LAST MEAL BEFORE THE
FAST

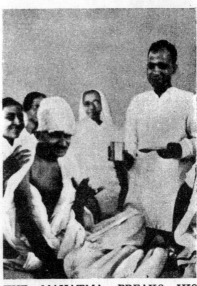

THE MAHATMA BREAKS HIS
FAST

THE HATER OF VIOLENCE

A picture taken of the Mahatma in 1939 still vigorously preaching his doctrine of non-aggressive methods and unity of effort.

crisis in order to compel her to grant India's freedom, that it would not be proper or generous on her part to take advantage of Britain's embarrassment in the international field, and his insistence that India must secure her substantial independence on her own merits and by her own united efforts.

The other is his uncompromising denunciation of widespread corruption within the Congress organisation and of the departure of large numbers of Congressmen from the method of truth and non-violence, laid down by the Congress at his instance as the fundamental tenet of its policy.

These are summarised in the following passage from a letter from Gandhi to Bose, in reply to the latter's proposed ultimatum, under threat of a new intensive civil disobedience campaign, just before his resignation, expressing Gandhi's profound disbelief that such

a campaign could be conducted without violence:

"I smell violence in the air I breathe. Our mutual distrust is a bad form of violence. The widening gulf between Hindus and Moslems points to the same thing."

It is too early yet to estimate finally Gandhi's influence upon his Motherland or upon world events; but it may be truly said that to him, more than to any predecessor or contemporary, is due the vivid national consciousness of India to-day and the growing respect in which she is held abroad. To many he is a strange enigma, an aggregate of inconsistencies, and his subtlety of argument is often incomprehensible and baffling. But of his courage, his integrity of purpose, the splendour of his idealism, his deep patriotism, and his fine example of public conduct and personal sacrifice there is an all but universal recognition.

PUNDIT MOTILAL NEHRU

PUNDIT MOTILAL NEHRU

A MAKER OF MODERN INDIA

1861–1931

BY C. F. ANDREWS

PUNDIT MOTILAL NEHRU belonged to that older generation of great men in India, of which Rabindranath Tagore is to-day one of the very few now living. It is a curious fact that Motilal's birthday came on exactly the same day of the year and month as that of the poet: for he was born on May 6, 1861.

Among his contemporaries, in Allahabad, Pundit Madan Mohan Malaviya comes nearest to him in age. Dr. Brajendranath Seal, that giant of massive learning in Bengal, who has just passed away, was somewhat younger. Sir Prafulla Chandra Roy, the renowned chemist, is about the same age as Rabindranath Tagore. Sir Jagadish Chandra Bose was a contemporary. Sir Nilratan Sarkar, who is still with us, belongs to the same generation. Lala Lajpat Rai in the Punjab was younger. Many names might be recalled in other provinces, but space will hardly allow it. What I have tried to point out is that the "sixties" of last century produced a larger number of eminent men than the years that followed. It must not be forgotten that Mahatma Gandhi himself comes just within this period.

Kashmiri Brahmans, to which class Pundit Motilal Nehru belonged, are well known all over the north of India both for their intellectual powers and fine appearance. They are, by birth, what may truly be called an aristocratic race, and easily recognised as such. Motilal was typical of this distinguished class and in his old age he gained the reputation of being the "aristocrat of the Assembly." His spotless *khaddar*

dress, with his white Kashmiri shawl, suited him perfectly, and his portrait is rightly given the place of honour in his son's Autobiography. The fine features—which I have mentioned—and the fair complexion run through the whole family, and have descended from father to son.

Although, as a boy, Motilal took little interest in his school and college studies he was from an early age keenly interested in the subject of law. He came out first as "Gold medallist" in the High Court Vakil's examination and showed at once his marked ability. His father had died three months before he was born, so that he never knew what it was to have a father. But his elder brother, Nandlal, who was much older than himself, took the place of a father towards him during his school and college days and afterwards introduced him into his own practice at the Bar. This brother, however, died very early in Motilal's legal career and thus he was soon thrown upon his own resources.

According to the immemorial custom of India, Motilal was now obliged to bear the burden of all the members of the family who were settled in Allahabad. This meant very hard work at his legal profession, from morning to night, building up his practice. But he thoroughly enjoyed it and very rapidly climbed the ladder which led to success.

All the facts which I have thus briefly related are to be found in the remarkable Autobiography written by his son, Jawaharlal, who was for many years his only child. Much later in life two daughters were also born to him, and these three made up his family. But under the same roof there were a large number of cousins and near relatives, who formed a joint family together in the spacious house called Anand Bhavan.

It was there, at Anand Bhavan, that I first met Motilal Nehru more than thirty years ago. A family residence of this type is like the ancestral house of a clan in the Highlands of Scotland. Everyone who is a near relative, and also the servants who grow up in it, regard themselves as members of the joint family. The memory of my first meeting with Pundit Motilal Nehru is very dim to-day; but I can easily picture the house where he lived and his very handsome appearance. Delhi and Allahabad were closely associated in their intellectual life in those times. There was a close fellowship also between Moslems and Hindus within the different intellectual groups. The common Urdu language, in which very great pride was taken by both Hindus and Moslems, bound them together. The Western culture, which had come also into fashion, was another link common to this very small circle of English-educated people. The members of leading families met continually, especially at marriages. My own educational work soon brought me into touch with Allahabad and also with Anand Bhavan.

Motilal Nehru was from the first quite lavish in his hospitality. More and more he had adopted, after each visit to Europe, the expensive standard of living common in the West. Exceedingly foolish stories about his Western habits were spread widely over the north of India, which were ridiculous to those who knew him in his own house; for whatever he did in this direction, as events proved, was merely on the surface, and could be thrown off at a moment's notice. He frankly admired the character of the Englishmen he met who had been trained in the English public schools. Therefore he sent his only son to Harrow, and never regretted that action. But all through his life he was far too deeply wedded to his own country and its traditions to make him ever forget his birthright.

When I first came to know him intimately was in the autumn of 1919 at Amritsar and Lahore, where we met together during the first days of the Congress Enquiry into the Punjab disturbances and the acts which had been committed under martial law.

His son, Jawaharlal Nehru, had come up alone, in the first instance, immediately after martial law had been withdrawn and the entry into the Punjab had become possible. We had lived together for some time at Harkishen Lal's house in Lahore before any one else arrived. Each day, when we came back from one disturbed area after another, we used to compare notes in the evening. Then Motilal Nehru himself came, as soon as he was free from his engagements. Mahatma Gandhi soon followed, when the order against him was withdrawn. It was painful to witness how shock after shock went home, when they both examined, as trained lawyers, the evidence which we put before them. Some of the worst things that were done under martial law were not done in Amritsar or in Lahore, but in the Gujranwala district, in villages whose names even were quite unknown. It was a lesson that I never forget to notice how very carefully they sifted the evidence, and at once put aside as untrustworthy all that I had collected, at second-hand, on hearsay only.

Long before this Enquiry was over, the more urgent call suddenly came to me to go out to Kenya and South Africa.

I was very sorry to go away, but before I left the Punjab a golden opportunity had been given me of seeing at first-hand those two leaders of India, as they then were, closely associated together in this common investigation on behalf of those who had suffered under martial law.

That memorable year 1919, in Indian history, changed once and for all the mode of life of Pundit Motilal Nehru. Before this time, as we have seen, he had made some of his closest friends in Europe, and also among the ruling classes in India who were British by race and tradition. He greatly admired that tradition, while holding himself free to criticise it. He had also many friends among the aristocracy of India. His whole mind had been steeped in law and constitutional government. Though he had been for some time a member of the Congress, he had always represented the Right rather than the Left. But Amritsar shook the very foundations of the faith on which he had built up his life hitherto; and when he presided over the National Congress, which was held at Amritsar that very year, 1919, he felt that the parting of the ways had come between him and his old liberal friends. Then, when at last the call came to join the Non-Co-operation Movement, under the leadership of Mahatma Gandhi, he was fully prepared to accept it. He did this slowly and deliberately, realising all the consequences which it involved.

He would have been the first to acknowledge that, in his own home, there were those on both sides of the family—the women no less than men —who were eager to help him to make this great decision to join Mahatma Gandhi. Then, as soon as he had made it, the whole family became united. Jawaharlal's mother and wife and daughter took part in the struggle side by side with Motilal Nehru himself and his son.

Yet there was a marked difference from the very first that soon revealed itself. Motilal Nehru, as I have just said, was quite obviously inclined to the Right in all his actions and decisions. Even after he had joined the Non-Co-operation Movement this continued. So, after the first flush of the new venture of Non-Co-operation was over and it became logically evident to him that he could win more power by entering the Central Legislative Assembly, he was prepared to do this along with his great friend C. R. Das of Bengal. He was thus led materially to differ from Mahatma Gandhi. Those who followed the latter were called No-changers. As a parallel organisation, the Swaraj Party was formed by Motilal Nehru and C. R. Das. The parliamentary methods of obstruction, which Parnell and his Irishmen had so brilliantly tried out at Westminster, were put into execution at Delhi.

The next time I met Pundit Motilal Nehru was at Juhu, near Bombay, where Mahatma Gandhi was recovering from his very serious operation in the Sassoon Hospital at Poona. He came and stayed at Juhu for some time in order to be near Mahatmaji and talk things over; and I had many opportunities of seeing the lighter side of his character as the two leaders together made great fun of one another. Mahatmaji was convalescent and recovering health. He was thus in a joking mood with everyo\... The whole Nehru family was in residence at Juhu during those extraordinary days, while Motilal and Gandhi talked out—as it seemed to me, almost interminably—the pros and cons of "Council Entry." Neither convinced the other; but, meanwhile, in the intervals between these long conversations, I had got to know Pundit

Motilal Nehru very much better than I had ever done before. I was also able to witness and appreciate his deep admiration for Mahatma Gandhi as a man. As a "Mathama" he was far less interested in him; but that made everything between them more human. He would chaff Gandhi mercilessly and nothing pleased him better. I wish I could remember some of the jokes, which were of a very elementary character, but they have quite passed from me. Just one I recollect, how he called Mahatma Gandhi "a bit of a dandy" because of his spotlessly white *khaddar!* Behind all the merriment, however, was a firmness on both sides which became at times crucially painful because the two minds, so strongly dissimilar, would not always work together. Yet the affection between them became all the deeper because of their very differences.

The portrait drawn by Jawaharlal of his father is one of the finest descriptions in his Autobiography.[1] "There was in him," he writes, "a strength of personality and a measure of kingliness. In any gathering where he was present he would inevitably be the centre and the hub. Whatever the place he sat at table, it would become, as an eminent English judge said later, the head of the table. He was neither meek nor mild. Consciously imperious, he created great loyalty as well as bitter opposition. It was difficult to feel neutral about him; one had to like him or dislike him. With a broad forehead, tight lips, and a determined chin he had a marked resemblance to the busts of the Roman Emperors in the museums in Italy. There was a magnificence about him and a grand manner, which is sadly to seek in this world of to-day.

"I remember," he adds, "showing Gandhiji a photograph of him, where

he had no moustache, and till then Gandhiji had always seen him with a fine moustache. He started almost on seeing this photograph and gazed long upon it; for the absence of the moustache brought out the hardness of the mouth and chin; and he said with a somewhat dry smile that now he realised what he had to contend against. The face was softened, however, by the eyes and by the lines that frequent laughter had made. But sometimes the eyes glittered."

In all my own memories of him this gentler side predominated, and I remember him chiefly by his lavish fund of humour and his eagerness to engage in a bout of wit and merriment especially with Gandhiji himself. Yet no one admired Gandhi more than Motilal Nehru. "That humble and lonely figure," he wrote about him, "standing erect, on the firm footholds of faith unshakable and strength unconquerable, continues to send out to his countrymen his message of sacrifice and suffering for the Motherland."

On other later occasions it has been my privilege to see these two together, each great in his own way, but strongly dissimilar; and it has made me understand more clearly how this affection for Mahatma Gandhi has descended from father to son. Indeed, the whole Nehru family has joined in it.

The great event in the earlier days of Non-Co-operation, for which Pundit Motilal Nehru and Chittaranjan Das were responsible, became known as "Council Entry." They had argued out to the bitter end with Mahatmaji the value of the movement, if they went boldly into the Councils as Parnell the Irish leader did fifty years ago in England, and thus obstructed the Government within the legislatures.

At last Mahatmaji gave way; and at the next elections the Swaraj Party, as it was called, was fully organised and every-

[1] *An Autobiography*, pages 130 and 131, *published by John Lane, Bodley Head, London.*

where carried the polls. When Motilal Nehru was chosen to be leader of the opposition in the Central Assembly at New Delhi, as the head of the Swaraj Party, he felt himself once more entirely in his own element. He was no longer like a fish out of water. His whole legal training and his knowledge of assemblies had all along made him anxious to engage in a battle royal with the Imperial Government, using its own weapons to defeat it. He was quite certain that he could bring it down to its knees.

In this opinion he was more or less justified; for the Government suffered outwardly defeat after defeat at his hands. Indeed, on all the larger issues, it could only rely on its own official and nominated members, and these, by themselves, were not sufficient to form a majority. But his triumphs proved to be Pyrrhic victories after all, because as soon as ever any Government measure was defeated it was at once certificated by the Viceroy. There was also a majority ready in the Upper House to reverse the decision of the Assembly.

A subtle danger, meanwhile, attacked the Swaraj Party. For every possible inducement was given to its members to serve on one Committee after another, or to take this post or that, bringing certain emoluments with them. When these were accepted, the full force of a revolutionary method of procedure was continually frustrated.

During these difficult years, Pundit Motilal Nehru undertook almost alone the immensely arduous task of drawing up a form of constitution, by which India should have full Dominion Status within the British Commonwealth. His son, Jawaharlal, could not endure the limited terms on which this constitution was being framed, because they did not make absolutely clear that India's full independence was the goal. A considerable amount of friction arose between father

and son on this issue and a compromise was reached at last with great difficulty, whereby the offer to accept this "Dominion Status" constitution would expire at the end of the year 1929.

It will not be possible to write much about the later years of his life during which he had to suffer imprisonment for taking an active part in the Civil Resistance Movement along with many other members of his family. Long before he took part in the struggle he had been afflicted for very many years with an acute form of asthma, which caused him great physical pain and put a severe strain upon his heart. But his utterly resolute temperament would not allow him for a moment to stand by while others suffered, even though he was already to all intents and purposes an invalid and had reached his 70th year.

In the jail, his illness rapidly grew worse, and it was obvious that prison life was doing him untold injury, because he could get no proper treatment for his asthma and heart trouble, under jail conditions. Yet he became immediately angry if anyone suggested that he should be released because of his infirmities. He went to the length of sending a telegram to the Viceroy, Lord Irwin, saying that he did not wish to claim any exemption. But on the doctors' imperative orders he was discharged after exactly ten weeks' imprisonment.

Then came the fifth arrest of his only son, Jawaharlal. The old father pulled himself together and declared to every one present that he was going to be ill no longer. For a time his indomitable spirit prevailed; but after a short period the blood came back into his sputum in greater quantities than ever. Therefore, he was urged to go to Calcutta for the purpose of taking a sea voyage along with a friend who was a doctor: but his condition so quickly grew worse that he could not make his journey any further than Calcutta. Yet even then his will was quite unconquerable, and he carried forward every part of his civil resistance just as before.

He returned to Allahabad, and his son Jawaharlal was discharged a little while before the others in order to be with him. Mahatma Gandhi had also been discharged at Yeravda and many others among the Congress leaders. These came to Allahabad and were able to meet him, one by one, for the last time before his death.

"I am going soon," he said to Mahatma Gandhi, "and I shall not be here to see Swaraj. But I know that you have won it."

The end came on February 6th. For many millions, in every part of India, it seemed as if a dear personal friend had been taken from them. His son writes:

"I was dazed all that day, hardly realising what had happened, and a succession of events and large crowds kept me from thinking. Great crowds in Lucknow, gathered together at brief notice—the swift dash from Lucknow to Allahabad sitting by the body, wrapped in our national flag, and with a big flag flying above—the arrival at Allahabad, and the huge crowds that had gathered for miles to pay homage to his memory. There were some ceremonies at home, and then the last journey to the Ganga with a mighty concourse of people. As evening fell on the river bank on that winter day, the great flames leapt up and consumed that body which had meant so much to us, who were close to him, as well as to millions in India. Gandhiji

MRS. VIJAYALAXMI PANDIT
Daughter of Motilal Nehru and herself prominent in politics.

said a few moving words to the multitude and then all of us crept silently home. The stars were out and shining brightly when he returned, lonely and desolate."

Messages came pouring in from every side—from those who had been his most stalwart opponents in the Assembly, from the Viceroy and Lady Irwin, as well as from those dear companions who had stood side by side with him in the civil resistance campaign.

"This tremendous volume of goodwill and sympathy" wrote Jawaharlal, "took away somewhat the sting from our sorrow; but it was, above all, the wonderfully soothing and healing presence of Gandhiji that helped my mother and all of us to face that crisis in our lives."

Looking back after all these years, it has now become evident to thinking men all over the world that the good fight which Motilal Nehru fought was carried through to the end with a chivalry and courtesy towards his opponents that made his cause truly great and noble. His name is honoured to-day in India, not only by his fellow countrymen, but also by every European. In his own career, as a statesman he stands out more prominently than ever, as one who brought the debates of the Central Assembly at Delhi to a higher parliamentary level than has ever been reached before or since. Certainly no one has ever been so great as he, as Leader of the Opposition. In this, and in a thousand other ways, he has been one of the "Makers of Modern India."

PUNDIT JAWAHARLAL NEHRU

The Ex-President of Congress in a characteristic attitude delivering a speech.

PUNDIT JAWAHARLAL NEHRU

THE CHAMPION OF THE INDIAN PEOPLE

BORN 1889

BY C. F. ANDREWS

PUNDIT JAWAHARLAL NEHRU has made any description of his own personality comparatively simple because he has published one of the most revealing books of modern times, which tells us the story of his own life. It is a natural temptation, therefore, for one who is writing about him to draw largely from the book itself. But while I shall not fail to make use of what he has himself written, I shall seek at the same time to add other features from my own recollections.

Yet, before doing so, I would wish to dwell for a moment on the *Autobiography* itself, which has proved such an amazing success. It was issued from the press in London in April, 1936, and by August of the same year the eighth impression had been printed off. These first sales were mainly in England, and it was there that its great reputation was made. The equally large sales in India came later. New editions are still being published, which show that the book will continue to live when others are forgotten.

It was the entire frankness of what was written, together with the profound interest of the story he told, that gained Jawaharlal his very large and important reading public. He had the great advantage of being able to speak to the intellectual classes—especially at the Universities—in the very phrases and terms which they themselves used. He wrote as one of themselves. He told Englishmen exactly what they wanted to know about India in his own transparently clear style, and made them feel that India was not merely a land of

saints and mystics but also of quite human and fallible people like himself, who were definitely lined up to fight against Hitler and Mussolini along with any freedom-loving Englishman, if only the latter would allow the same freedom to India that he demanded for himself.

"Here's a man we can understand," was the remark that a young civilian made on his first voyage out to India. "He's one of ourselves after all, and talks to us in our own language."

Probably more was accomplished in a few months by this one volume to swing round liberal opinion in the West than had been accomplished by the many years of political struggle that had gone before.

It is true that the strong impression which had been made by these multiple editions could hardly be lasting. Europe to-day is in such a turmoil and confusion that even the most liberal-minded Englishmen are inclined to cry out, "We have no time for India." But the pendulum is bound to swing back later and some new incident will bring India once more into the forefront of the picture. Then the same people, who had read the book before with such eagerness, will turn to the copy which is on their shelves and read through over again Jawaharlal's prophetic warnings.

Another point must not be overlooked. The remarkable photographs which have been reproduced have themselves proved to be a revelation to the ordinary reader. The frontispiece of Pundit Motilal Nehru, the father of the author, looking in his "toga" like someone out of the ancient Roman Empire; the face of the author himself, showing the markedly strong and clear-cut character that lies behind it; above all, perhaps, the tender portraits of the mother, wife and daughter of the author, disclosing a perfect refinement mingled with true womanly courage—all these tell their own story. Every English reader, as he turns over the pages, becomes in his heart of hearts ashamed that persons such as these should have been obliged to go to prison in order to make their voices heard. Thus the portraits have given rise to some very painful thinking. They have shown that all is not right in India. This last factor, as I know full well, has very deeply touched the women of England, who have recently gained, by a hard struggle, their own political rights. The women's influence in England to-day is no less important than that of the men, and their full weight is being thrown more and more on the side of Indian freedom.

One of Jawaharlal Nehru's most bitter opponents in the United Provinces, a diehard and a reactionary, paid him in my hearing a compliment, which is well worth quoting at this point. For it sums up a great deal.

"Whatever," he said, "we may think of young Nehru's socialistic doctrines and his Bolshevist ideas, the efficient way in which he handled the Allahabad Municipality, as Chairman, was beyond all praise."

This practical efficiency in all he undertakes and his clean contempt for shoddy work, have won him esteem from those who have heartily disliked his politics. The same people have also admired the out-spokenness with which he has been ready at all times to acknowledge faults of character and weakness of purpose within himself and others. This feature in his character has won him universal respect.

Among the multitudes of his own people, who love him with a devotion second only to that of Mahatmaji himself, the same quality of supreme honesty tells for very much. It endears him to them. But along with this, the conviction that he has never hesitated for a moment to suffer with them, and on their behalf, tells for even more. In the United Provinces there has grown up, year by year, a simple loyalty of devotion towards him among the villagers that is absolute in character.

I recollect his telling me once, at Allahabad, with a certain amount of dry humour, the story of the way in which he tried to train the ignorant villagers of his own province in the pure doctrine of non-violence, which they persistently failed to understand.

"What would you do," he asked a group of village leaders, "if you saw me taken prisoner before your very eyes and then handcuffed by the police?"

"We would rush in and rescue you," they replied at once in chorus.

"No, no," said Jawaharlal, "that's just what you mustn't do! You must keep perfectly calm and quiet. You mustn't move a step."

They would stare at him with a singularly puzzled look and he would patiently go on to tell them that even if they saw him beaten with *lathis*, they were not to use any violence in return. For these things were only to be expected.

"But we couldn't bear it," they shouted.

"You've *got* to bear it," was the answer.

And so the lesson in *Ahimsa* would have to begin all over again until it was learnt by heart.

The greatest strain of all came, in the United Provinces, when his own aged mother was injured by the police.

PUNDIT JAWAHARLAL AS PRESIDENT

A photograph taken of Jawaharlal Nehru when he was President of Congress. He is seen on the extreme right presiding over a Special Meeting of the All-India Convention Subjects Committee. Facing the camera are K. Munshi, Mrs. Hansa Mehta, Jairamdas Daulatram.

Jawaharlal himself was in prison at the time.

He frankly acknowledges, in his book, that if he had been on the spot, his Ahimsa might have been put to too severe a strain!

The deeply touching faith which these villagers repose in him I have witnessed personally again and again in all sorts of ways.

At the first, on his return from London and Cambridge, they had little chance of coming into very close contact with him; for he was incessantly occupied with various city engagements in Allahabad and also with his lawyer's work at the Bar. But from the moment when he gave himself up, heart and soul, to the Non-Co-operation Movement and placed himself with absolute loyalty and devotion under the leadership of Mahatma Gandhi, this old life of his began to be changed. The villagers now were made more and more his chief concern.

He worked with them, lived with them, and thus learnt to understand their tragic struggle against overwhelming odds. He knew them now at close quarters. So he won their hearts and they won his.

The book that he has written gives many touching indications of this, from which I would quote the following passage:

"There they were, these people, looking up with their shining eyes, full of affection, with generations of suffering and poverty behind them, and still pouring out their gratitude and love, and asking for little in return, except fellow-feeling and sympathy. It was impossible not to feel humbled and awed by this abundance of affection and devotion."

Mainly on account of his personal leadership and that of his own devoted companions, the *Kisan*, or Peasant Movement, in the United Provinces has become strongly organised and powerful. The only province that comes near it is Bihar, where Rajendra Prasad has won a similar confidence among his own countrymen.

It is of the utmost importance to realise this radical change which has come over the whole Congress Movement since the leadership was given into the hands of Mahatma Gandhi nearly twenty years ago. Before that time even leaders like Jawaharlal Nehru and his father thought in English, spoke in English, regarded the Congress itself as an organ of English opinion which had to deal chiefly with what was called "Educated India" and its disabilities. But just at the crucial moment, when everything was at stake and a leader for all India was needed, Mahatma Gandhi came to the front in such a manner that for the time being he united all the progressive forces in a compact body and received the whole-hearted allegiance not only of Motilal and Jawaharlal Nehru, but also of men like C. R. Das, J. M. Sen Gupta, Dr. Ansari, Maulana Muhammad Ali, Madan Mohan Malaviya, and others, whose outlook hitherto had been confined for the most part to the rights of citizenship for the small educated minority to which they belonged. The ninety per cent. of village India had only come indirectly into their political horizon.

But Mahatma Gandhi, living himself the life of a poor peasant, soon changed all that and brought those who sought his political support face to face with realities. The village now became the centre of the picture: its needs were India's needs; its language must be India's language.

Jawaharlal Nehru was among the very first to recognise this drastic change that was coming over the whole scene. He began to work out, with some compunction, what it would mean in detail to his own manner of living. Quite inevitably it would imply giving up many expensive habits and coming nearer to the level of those for whom he was now destined to work day and night.

It is easy to see from his autobiography how at first he half resisted some of these practical conclusions. When I was with him in Lala Harkishen Lal's house in Lahore, in 1919, after the humiliations under martial law, the change had only just begun. But what he met with in the Punjab—the horror of it—hastened the process, as did also the golden opportunity of seeing a great deal of Mahatma Gandhi during those days. No one could be with him at that time, in his entire physical exhaustion combined with amazing spiritual strength, without searching himself through and through.

But there was an honest revolt also, which this book by Jawaharlal clearly indicates. There was in him no blind worship. For he is a "modern," with no liking whatever for the extreme ascetic practices of Mahatma Gandhi. Mere fasts and penances do not attract him. They only irritate him, when they take the strange forms that mediæval saints practised. For they seem to him to be irrational. Thus his twentieth century mind had prevented him hitherto from carrying out to the full many of the things which seem to appeal with irresistible force to Mahatma Gandhi.

And yet the massive simplicity of Gandhi draws Jawaharlal all the while nearer and nearer to his own standard. He quotes more than once that striking phrase where Gandhi describes his aim as *"Complete identification with the poorest of mankind, longing to live no better than they."*

If a sheer record were taken of all that Jawaharlal has suffered in the last twenty years, since Non-Co-operation was started, it would be seen to come not far short of Gandhi's own extreme privations which have brought him so close to the hearts of the poor people. No one, for instance, can fail to be struck by the way in which the moment

Jawaharlal has been set free from prison he is at once courting another arrest by some action which he cannot avoid if he would be true to his own principles. To give an example, the Bihar Earthquake happens soon after he is set free. So, after making a challenging speech in Calcutta directly after his release, he takes the next train and is on the spot, toiling night and day among the terror-stricken village people. Only then, when he has done all he possibly could, does he return home. "I got back," he writes, "dead tired after my tour. Ten strenuous days had made me look ghastly and my people were surprised at my appearance. I tried to begin writing my report, but sleep overcame me. So I spent at least twelve out of the next twenty-four hours in sleep. Next day, Kamala and I had just finished tea, when a car drove up and a police officer alighted. I knew immediately my time had come."

It is a hard doctrine, this "complete identification with the poorest of mankind," which Mahatmaji has laid down as the true "democratic test." Yet who can doubt that those who come nearest to it in practice are able finally to win the loyalty and love of the masses of simple village people in India, who judge by deeds not words?

"Whether Gandhiji," writes Jawaharlal, "is a democrat or not, he does represent the peasant masses of India; he is the quintessence of the conscious and subconscious will of those millions. It is perhaps something more than representation: for he is the idealised personification of

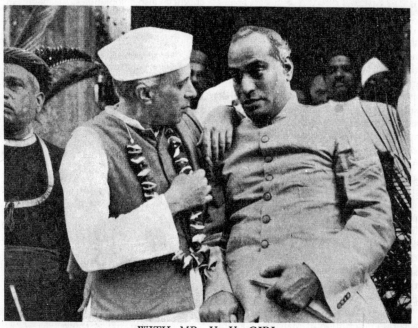

WITH MR. V. V. GIRI

A serious discussion between Pundit S. Nehru and the Hon. V. V. Giri during a meeting in Bombay.

THE LEADER
Pundit Nehru addressing a Congress Meeting at Lucknow.

that Gandhi makes to all the leading spirits in India who come within the close range of his personal influence and are ready to respond to its call.

"I have been," writes Jawaharlal in another remarkable passage about himself, "a queer mixture of the East and West, out of place everywhere, at home nowhere. Perhaps my thoughts and approach to life are more akin to what is called Western than Eastern, but India clings to me, as she does to all her children, in innumerable ways. I cannot get rid of that past inheritance of my recent acquisitions. They are both part of me, and, though they help me in both the East and the West, they create in me a feeling of spiritual loneliness not only in public activities, but in life itself. I am a stranger and alien in the West. I cannot be of it. But in my own country also, sometimes, I have an exile's feeling."

Yet out of all this inner conflict there

those vast millions. Of course, he is not the average peasant. A man of the keenest intellect, of fine feeling and good taste, wide vision; very human, and yet essentially the ascetic, who has suppressed his passions and emotions, sublimated them and directed them in spiritual channels; a tremendous personality, drawing people to himself like a magnet, and calling out fierce loyalties and attachments—all this so utterly unlike and beyond a peasant. And yet withal he is the great peasant, with a peasant's blindness to some aspects of life. But India is peasant India; and so he knows his India well and reacts to her lightest tremors, and gauges a situation accurately and almost instinctively, and has a knack of acting at the psychological moment."

In every phrase of this remarkably accurate description of Mahatma Gandhi we can see how the author has been attracted by the extraordinary appeal

AT LUCKNOW
Speaking into a microphone as he presides over the meeting.

WOMEN TAKE THEIR PART IN NATIONAL LIFF

A procession of the All-India Women's League in Calcutta. Pundit Jawaharlal, whose sister was a member of Congress, encourages Indian women to take part in political affairs.

12

has come the power which has made him the one great driving force in national India, second only to Mahatma Gandhi. His attitude towards the latter oscillates but always comes back to the same centre. He is severely critical, yet at the same time won over to admiration and affection. He is continually repelled, and yet he realises that in the very things that jar upon him lies the secret of Gandhi's power with the vast multitudes of simple village people.

On one salient point there is no difference between them. For they both realise that only by infinite sacrifice and suffering can India's freedom be attained. And Jawaharlal knows absolutely that this one frail man, who has so often put his own life at stake, has won his way to India's heart as no one else has ever done, and that he alone can lead India forward to the final goal of Swaraj.

This increasing consciousness of the fate of the multitudes, in India, of poverty-stricken people has also drawn Jawaharlal Nehru irresistibly towards what he calls "Socialism." But in using this general word he is no doctrinaire, and has nothing but contempt for "arm-chair" economists, who seek to gain a cheap notoriety by using catch phrases. He knows intimately the difference between Indian conditions and those of the West. What changes are to be made in India must be made from the standpoint of Indian economy, not that of Europe.

Yet, while he recognises these practical differences, he is desperately in earnest about the immediate need in India of revolution in the economic and social system now prevailing. Whether it is in the petty Indian States, or in the large landlord areas, or in the mill centres, the concentration of arbitrary power in the

AT LUDHIANA

The men's procession during the All-India States' People's Conference at Ludhiana in 1939.

hands of a single person, who for all practical purposes has powers of life and death over thousands of helpless people, has become intolerable to him just in the same way that the imperialism of foreign rule has become intolerable also. He has seen this vision of the suffering peasant in India and other lands, and in a socialist co-operative endeavour, whereby the land and the instruments of production are placed at the service of the community, he sees the way out of this inveterate evil.

He quotes the moving lines of the American poet, E. Markham, from "The Man with the Hoe":

> "Bowed by the weight of
>   centuries he leans
>   Upon his hoe and gazes
>   on the ground,
> The emptiness of ages on
>   his face,
> And on his back the burden of the
>   world.

> "Through this dread shape the suffering
>   ages look.
> Time's tragedy is in that aching stoop,
> Through this dread shape humanity
>   betrayed,
> Plundered, profaned and disinherited,
> Cries protest to the powers that made
>   the world,
> A protest that is also prophecy."

IN CALCUTTA

Pundit Jawaharlal Nehru being driven through the crowded streets in a flower-decked carriage.

Strangely enough, at this very point, Jawaharlal, having gone thus far with Mahatma Gandhi, and having half accepted his hard doctrine of "complete identification with the poorest of mankind," parts company with him as to the methods to be employed for bringing the present evils to an end.

Mahatmaji, on his side, is willing to allow the rajah and the money-lender, and the Zamindar and the mill-owner to go on with their personal rule over those who are economically in their power provided the one religious quality of divine charity (which he would call *Ahimsa*) can be introduced into their despotic sway and thus cause it to become, for the time being at any rate, a "Rama Rajya"—a Kingdom of God upon earth. But Jawaharlal, on the other side, can see no lasting remedy in such a personal change in the heart of a single rajah, or Zamindar or mill-owner.

A RECENT STUDY OF PUNDIT JAWAHARLAL NEHRU

He regards the whole system of despotic power, whether brought about by capitalism or imperialism, as an evil in itself. He believes that some form of co-operative ownership of land and of the instruments of production must in the end lead to more equitable and stable results.

Thus the soul of Jawaharlal is vexed within him when he sees Mahatma Gandhi holding out the hand of cordial friendship and even partnership to those whose very function in society he believes to be destructive of elementary justice. Gandhiji, on the other hand, has

SEEKING GANDHI'S ADVICE
Jawaharlal Nehru climbing the stairs to the Mahatma's apartment to consult with him.

his eyes fixed on the inner conversion of the rajah and the landlord and the moneylender and the capitalist which may lead them to a voluntary surrender of their power.

Looking back over what I have now written, I can see that I have attempted an impossible task in trying to compress into one brief article the life story of one of the greatest living personalities of the modern age. Nevertheless, if I have left a vivid picture of the inner struggle of one who is still young in years though old in wisdom and sorrow, I shall be content.

SIR FAZL-I-HUSAIN

SIR FAZL-I-HUSAIN

THE PUNJAB'S POLITICAL LEADER AND REFORMER
1877–1936

BY SIR GEORGE ANDERSON, C.S.I., C.I.E.

THE early career of Fazl-i-Husain ran along normal lines. After graduating from the University of the Punjab, and later of Cambridge, he was called to the Bar and subsequently built up a good, though by no means an exceptional, practice in the Punjab. In common with many other Indian politicians he took a deep interest in education, and the fortunes of Islamia College, Lahore, owed much to his perseverance and loyalty. He was for many years a member both of the Senate and Syndicate of Punjab University; and he also represented that university on the Legislative Council of the province. In politics he was what may be termed a progressive nationalist and he soon earned the reputation of being a staunch critic and opponent of the old-time bureaucracy. Had events pursued a different course he might, along with many others of his political associates, have found himself in gaol as a political offender. Had this been his lot, he would assuredly have met his fate with stoical indifference and with cynical contempt.

The institution of the Montagu-Chelmsford reforms, however, marked the turning point of his career. In 1921 he became Education Minister in the Punjab and, after a few years, he was transferred to the post of Revenue Member. He later served for five years as Education Member in the Government of India. Thus he held high office continuously for a period of fifteen years. Subsequent to his retirement in 1936 he returned to his home in Lahore and at once busied himself in the politics of the province. Had his life been spared, there can be little doubt that he would have been the first Premier of the Punjab.

Such, in brief, is the story of Fazl-i-Husain. But, eminent though his services undoubtedly were, his record, by itself, was scarcely such as to justify his inclusion in this series of the *Great Men of India;* and there are further considerations which deepen our perplexity as to his correct place in the history of India.

Though he was often effective in debate and though at times he spoke with force and persuasion, especially in the vernacular, he was not possessed of oratorical talent. His voice was lacking both in power and resonance, and the thread of his argument was often broken by violent fits of coughing. He was incapable of inspiring others by the magic of the spoken word or by playing on the emotions of his listeners. It was not by set speeches that he could lead men to action.

Nor was he either an erudite scholar or a profound thinker. No learned book bears his name, and what little he wrote was largely ephemeral. Even the official files of the Lahore and Delhi secretariats contain little under his signature that betokens one who exercised, and whose memory to-day continues to exercise, widespread influence over men and things.

Though he was by no means lacking in kindness and though on many occasions he displayed great magnanimity and forbearance, often towards those who had little claim to expect generosity at his hands, he was scarcely an engaging personality. He was very reserved in his relations with others. Towards the end of his life, when his malady became ever more critical, he was extremely loath to leave his home and to seek the companionship of his fellow men. Though his circle of acquaintances was a very wide one, he had but few intimate friends. He made no personal appeal such as did Louis Botha, or does Stanley Baldwin. But he had more friends than he would have cared to admit; he certainly had more enemies than he had earned.

Let it also be remembered that for years before his death, at a comparatively early age, he suffered from a grievous malady which sapped his vitality. Scarcely a month passed but he was confined to his bed, and his temperature always appeared to be above normal. But his patience and optimism were heroic. While he resented commiseration, he rarely complained. Yet he continued to persevere until almost his last moments in planning for the future of India, and especially of the province which he had served so well. But in spite of his fortitude it became ever more evident to others that it would be hazardous to place much reliance on a life which had become so precarious.

In order to appreciate Fazl-i-Husain's correct contribution towards the life and progress of India it is necessary first to bear in mind the time and the place in which he lived.

It is difficult to regard the political reforms which bear the names of Mr. Edwin Montagu and Lord Chelmsford as providing an opportunity for anybody, however ingenious, to justify himself as one of the *Great Indians;* and, indeed, Fazl-i-Husain himself took no pains to conceal his view that those reforms were at best an unsatisfactory compromise. But it was his genius

and his political sagacity that enabled him to regard a difficult period of transition as the very time when preparations should be made for the next advance. That was the time when it should be proved that Indians were worthy of responsibility, and when all classes and communities should be encouraged and trained to make their full and effective contributions towards the development of the new India. The new India should not connote merely a particular class or community.

A narrow view of his policy would indicate, as many indeed held, that he thought merely of collecting the loaves and fishes for the benefit of the Moslem community. He undoubtedly spent much of his time in drawing up detailed figures regarding appointments and in fighting strenuously for communal percentages and quotas, but rarely did he seek appointments for particular individuals or even for those who were within his own circle. His object was rather that India should be enriched by the advance of all communities and should thereby live more abundantly.

Similarly, he was quick to realise, and was tenacious in the belief, that the strength and health of India lay in the countryside. The vast rural population of India should therefore be aided and encouraged to release themselves from the grave limitations imposed upon them by their own ignorance and by past neglect. If the life of India was to become pure and vigorous it should be strengthened by the attainments and self-reliance of those living in the villages.

Firm and steadfast in these beliefs, Fazl-i-Husain soon found welcome supporters from within the ranks of the bureaucracy with whom he was then brought into contact. Perhaps more than in any other province in India, the services in the Punjab have retained that

YOUNG MOHAMMEDANS IN SCHOOL
The School in the Mosque at Lahore.   Here the boys receive a general education as well as studying the Koran.

12*

A PUNJAB VILLAGE

A large proportion of the Punjab people are engaged in agriculture and live in villages such as this. It was for their betterment Sir Fazl-i-Husain chiefly worked.

devotion to the land and to the dwellers on the land, which had been implanted years before by Henry Lawrence; and that tradition has continued to be both potent and widespread. The life and training of many young civilians have pivoted round their settlement duties, which brought them into intimate contact with the lives and conditions of village folk. A further contact was provided by the feats of engineers who had built the great canals of the province, and by the resource of those who had come to live in the canal colonies. The Punjab was also "the sword-arm" of India; and many of those who had fought in the Great War had returned with their vision widened by contact with men and things in other lands. The influence of those men was permeating village life throughout the province.

Fazl-i-Husain was not himself the initiator of any great scheme of rural development. Indeed, the broad out-

lines of such a policy had been constructed and much had already been achieved. But it was he who saw the great opportunity and converted rural reform into a political reality.

There is much in his political career which resembles that of perhaps the most eminent and imaginative of English statesmen. After the memorable struggle with Robert Peel on the repeal of the corn duties, the Tory Party lost the services of most of its experienced supporters, and Benjamin Disraeli found himself at the head of a party bereft of leaders. It therefore became his lot to build up what ultimately became the modern Conservative Party and to impregnate it with his ideals; but he had to do so with most unpromising material. The land-owning classes have rarely been favourable to reform, whether it be religious or social, political or economic; and those classes in England were then smarting with indignation over what they conceived to have been the great betrayal. And in those early days Disraeli could scarcely have been regarded as one fitted to lead the land-owning aristocracy of England.

The distinguishing feature of Disraeli's policy was his intense love of England, especially of its countryside. He thought much of the strength and the might and the power of England, and these had sprung from the villages of England; the bowmen of Agincourt, the sea-dogs of Devon, the Ironsides of the eastern counties, the men who had fought and triumphed at Minden, Quebec and Waterloo. But Disraeli saw that with the dwindling of the countryside the strength and vitality of the race would be sapped. And he thought even more of the soul of England. With the

uncontrolled industrialisation of England there would inevitably ensue the sweated labour, the unhealthy conditions of vast industrial cities, a people stunted both in physical and in mental vigour. The very fibre of the race was at stake.

Fazl-i-Husain found himself in a somewhat similar position. His very acceptance of office had estranged him from most of his old political associates, who were brooding over what they also considered to have been their betrayal; and his very political astuteness enraged them almost beyond endurance. He had therefore to face a bitterly hostile legislative council and it was not long before he had to withstand, though successfully, a formal vote of no-confidence. And though there had been a large influx of rural members, few of these could be

THE PEOPLE OF THE PUNJAB

A group of Punjab village folk, typical people of this great agricultural province—the most important wheat growing area in India.

expected to stand up with success against opponents who were experienced in the thrust of debate and in political organisation. Mere voting strength, by itself, cannot prevail for long; it can quickly crumble in face of personal interest and intrigue as well as of alluring enticements from political opponents. To say the least, the prospects were far from promising.

Patience, imperturbability, attention to detail and, above all, political astuteness were the main gifts that Fazl-i-Husain brought to bear on his difficult task. He was himself an untiring worker, and everybody associated with him was also expected to work; to every one was given his allotted task. But for that task each had to be trained, and trained in the manner which his leader had devised for him. Diligence in voting was not enough.

As Fazl-i-Husain once expressed himself in his playful manner, he believed far more in tutorial classes than in mass lectures; in other words, the careful preparation for debates was of far greater importance than eloquent orations during debates. The real secret of his success was that even for discussion with an individual, and even more with a committee, he was always prepared. He knew exactly what he wanted and, what is more, he had carefully planned the very lines along which discussion should take place. The many who took part in such discussions will remember the untidy scraps of paper and the illegible hieroglyphics which prompted his memory and guided the trend of discussion. Every discussion, however unimportant it may have seemed to others, was to him a matter of supreme importance. And so it was that he usually got his way, and that not by peremptory commands but as a result of discussion. What was even more satisfactory, other people, and even the

writer of this article, also began to produce untidy scraps of paper.

But this endless round of discussions did not consist merely of interviews and committees with particular objects in view; he frequently gathered unto himself groups of his political supporters, often those who seemed to be of little value beyond the casting of their votes. But even they had to be taught to understand the barest rudiments of his policy. To them he expounded with infinite patience the pros and cons of each topic in turn; and how cavalierly would he brush aside any hasty expression of opinion before, as he put it, the right of holding an opinion had been earned by industry and thought!

He was at his best in preparing for a debate in the Legislature. He seemed to know by instinct the course which each debate would take. He knew that so-and-so would represent a particular point of view, and that point of view had to be countered. And often, by some astute move, would he lure his opponents into an untenable position to be exploited when his turn came to wind up the debate. Everything as far as possible had been pre-ordained, and so it was that he usually had his way also in debates.

Leaders had also to be brought into the foreground, but whence were they to be found? Fazl-i-Husain had a good eye for latent capacity. Perhaps his most faithful follower was Chaudhri (now Sir) Chhotu Ram, the leader of the Jat community in the eastern part of the province. His diligence and readiness of speech quickly responded to the encouragement which he received. There were also Captain (now Sir) Sikandar Hayat Khan, who later officiated with much distinction as Governor of the province and is now the first Premier of the Punjab; Malik (now Sir) Firoz Khan Noon, who served for many years as a minister in varying capacities and is now High Commissioner for India in London; and Sir Shahab-ud-din, who has been for many years President of the Legislature and has done much to model its practice and procedure on that of the House of Commons.

The most difficult task, however, was to ensure that the party should betoken its name, that it should seek to become national and to unite rather than divide the different sections and communities of the province. In its early days it took the form, perhaps inevitably, of being too exclusively a Moslem party, and political controversy was therefore conducted largely on communal lines. But by degrees the lines of cleavage tended to broaden and recruits from other communities were gladly enlisted. The fruits of Fazl-i-Husain's labours were reaped when the first Premier of the province was able to form a government, which was broad-based both in its leaders and in its rank and file. The anxious time of preparation had not been in vain.

The educational policy of Fazl-i-Husain was in close accord with his political policy; the encouragement of backward areas and of backward communities were its watchwords. It was natural therefore that he should pay particular attention to the needs of the countryside, and a rapid expansion of education in the villages was clearly indicated. But, in achieving that objective, he suffered from a dual handicap resulting from his past record and from his past inclinations.

It is a platitude that education should be a means of uniting and not of dividing the rising generation; but unfortunately the bane of education in the Punjab is its communal bias. Bearing in mind the acuteness of communal strife, it is tempting Providence that, from the age of early childhood until the time of early manhood, children should be educated in the narrowing atmosphere of a communal institution, but such had become very largely the accepted practice in the Punjab. It speaks much for the moral courage of Fazl-i-Husain that he strove to shake off early and valued associations and to do what he could to encourage the members of his community to send their children to publicly managed schools and colleges rather than to communal institutions. He therefore founded a large number of Government high schools throughout the province, and the support which he received from his community is indicated by the fact that in most of those schools there was a preponderance of Moslem pupils. The seed that he thus sowed is beginning already to bear fruit, and there is a growing desire among more thoughtful minds that the schools should be rescued from communal thraldom.

In the sphere of primary education Fazl-i-Husain had a more straightforward task. His policy was that of rapid expansion by means of schools maintained by local bodies. Hence it has come about that, whereas in Bengal the number of pupils attending *maktabs* approximates 800,000, the number in the Punjab is negligible. But it is doubtful whether Fazl-i-Husain realised sufficiently that, in view of the changing political situation, the position of local bodies needed review. He was apt in that respect to live in the past when he and his associates, in their struggle against the bureaucracy, regarded official interference with the activities of local bodies as anathema. Indian politicians, not unnaturally, have been slow to grasp the fact that ministerial responsibility and local independence go ill together. But an Education Minister must find it difficult to carry out his responsibility to the Legislature in the matter of education so long as almost unsupervised control is vested in inexperienced and sometimes corrupt local bodies. It is possible, however, that Fazl-i-Husain was aware of this anomaly and that he preferred to ease matters, as he often did, by personal discussions with those concerned rather than by introducing contentious legislation. He was a past-master in judging the pace of political advance and in gauging when the time for action had become ripe.

He was not content, however, with mere numerical progress. He was well aware of the grave defects from which education, especially in rural areas, was suffering. The writer of this article well remembers how, shortly after he had taken over the duties of Director of Public Instruction and Fazl-i-Husain himself had become Education Minister, a bulky file of papers was placed before him. It contained a mass of opinions indicating that as the distinction between Vernacular and Anglo-vernacular middle schools had become so slight, the Vernacular side of education should be merged in the Anglo-vernacular. The issue appeared to have been prejudged, and therefore the papers were forwarded with little comment to the minister. They were quickly returned with the observation that immediate discussion was imperative. In the course of that discussion the instructions of Fazl-i-Husain were both trenchant and decisive. He expressed in forcible terms the view that the abandonment of the Vernacular system would be fatal in many directions, notably in the further impoverishment of the countryside and in the further congestion of the schools and colleges in the towns.

As a result of his memorable intervention, the whole trend of educational policy as affecting rural areas was revolutionised. The number of Vernacular middle schools was rapidly advanced, farms and gardens were attached to them, teachers in agriculture were trained; and later, the whole teaching of the schools was brought into harmony with rural conditions and requirements.

But Fazl-i-Husain was not content. He saw clearly that if these schools were to hold their own with their Anglo-vernacular counterparts, they should lead to higher studies of a rural type. Unfortunately, he soon ceased to be Education Minister and the question was held in abeyance. The manner in which such higher studies should be provided has since become clearer owing to the increased attention now being paid to the urgent need of rural development. Schemes of rural reform, however, if imposed from without, are unlikely to achieve any lasting success; an indigenous agency is imperative. Social workers, both official and non-official, should be given training in a rural atmosphere; and for that training the preliminary teaching in Vernacular middle schools should provide an admirable foundation. As soon as suitable training in the rural social services has been instituted, Fazl-i-Husain's policy in rural education will have come to fruition.

Such is our appreciation of Fazl-i-Husain's place in Indian history. Though it was not gained by spectacular achievements, it was greatly to the benefit of India, and especially of the Punjab, that he lived and worked during the difficult, though important, period of transition which had been introduced by the Montagu-Chelmsford reforms.

Fazl-i-Husain's great contribution to the political development of India was that he believed heart and soul in discussion; especially since real and effective discussion is so often lacking in the life of India. In the schools and colleges teaching consists mainly of a succession of monologues by the teacher, which the students rarely understand and in which they themselves take but little part. Political programmes, again, are framed mainly by means of high-sounding resolutions passed unanimously and without discussion by gigantic meetings, in which the rank and file are expected only to assent and to applaud.

As has been shown in this article, Fazl-i-Husain's methods were different. He was a great political teacher, and few teachers have taken such devoted care over the training of their pupils. If it be true that genius consists in an infinite capacity for taking pains, then undoubtedly Fazl-i-Husain was a genius. A good teacher is not necessarily a profound thinker, and still less a great speaker; but rather one who can expound clearly and, far more important, can make his pupils think for themselves and do their full share of the work. As a result of Fazl-i-Husain's teaching, there is far more political thought and political reality in the Punjab than elsewhere in India.

IRRIGATION IN THE PUNJAB

The Lower Chenab Canal irrigating 1,800 square miles.

MAHOMED ALI JINNAH

MAHOMED ALI JINNAH

ORGANISER OF MOSLEM UNITY

BORN 1876

BY USMAN AHMAD ANSON

THE Government of India Act, 1935, will go down in the constitutional history of India as an event of the first importance. In itself it was an epoch-making event. But the years which preceded and followed it saw the operation of those processes which made Mahomed Ali Jinnah the unquestioned leader of the bulk of ninety million Moslems of India, and crystallised the policy which is associated with the name of Jinnah and of the All-India Moslem League. This, though the oldest political organisation of Moslems, had considerably lost strength and following owing to numerous and important secessions from its ranks. But on the eve of the introduction of the new Government of India Act, Mahomed Ali Jinnah revived and re-organised the Moslem League, and for all practical purposes set it on its feet again. Now he is the accepted and undisputed leader of the Moslem community and is its highly esteemed and deeply loved " Qaid-i-Azam." This was no sudden rise to greatness by a lucky combination of favourable circumstances, but the consummation of a long record of selfless service and devotion to the cause of India's freedom, and to the cause of the community to which he belongs and which has been and is bound to be a large and powerful factor in the shaping of the country's destiny.

Mahomed Ali Jinnah at the present day stands solely for the rights of the Moslem community. This fact is exploited by other parties and their leaders for making the allegation that Jinnah has become a reactionary and is an obstacle in the path of the country's freedom. That this is deliberate and calculated calumny on one of the most fearless and courageous patriots which India has produced will appear from a simple record of his career. Mahomed Ali Jinnah entered political life as a nationalist and a radical, but slowly and surely the force of events and tendencies and, above all, the uncompromising attitude of the majority veered him more and more towards his own community and the guardianship of its interests. It can be said without fear of contradiction that the Moslem community has not fared very well under the new reforms and if any organisation has greater claim on Jinnah's services than another, it is the All-India Moslem League. So far from being a stigma on Mahomed Ali Jinnah, his dissociation from the Indian National Congress and complete identification with the fortunes of the Moslem League is an object lesson to the students of history who may be interested in the reactions of minorities in politically unfree countries.

Sixty-three years ago there was a Christmas of special significance to the Moslems of India. It was the Christmas of the year 1876. It fell on a Sunday and whatever blessings and happiness it might have brought to the followers of the Christian faith, it certainly brought a blessing to the Moslems of India and happiness into a Moslem Khoja family of Karachi. On that day was born Mahomed Ali Jinnah to gladden the hearts of his lucky parents, being their first son. His father belonged to a mercantile community and was himself a wealthy merchant. But, luckily for Indian Moslems, he decided for his first son, Mahomed Ali, upon a career different from what the traditions of his community demanded. If he had followed the usual practice, Mahomed Ali would have been in his early years initiated into business and would have ended perhaps as a millionaire, perhaps a knight and a leader without any following. India would have lost a stout patriot, Moslems an able leader, and history one of its most interesting figures. But luckily his father chose to give him a liberal education and make him a barrister.

Mahomed Ali Jinnah had his early education at Karachi. In 1892, at the tender age of sixteen, he was sent out to England by his parents. Fortunately for himself and for India the contacts which he made at this impressionable age were of the healthiest character and necessarily played their part in the formative process which made the Jinnah of later years. Above all he met about this time Dadabhai Naoroji, who saw with his experienced eye that this lad of 17, if properly influenced and guided, would go far indeed. Dadabhai Naoroji, already a veteran of mature years, was at that time President of the Indian Society in London. His is the first name in the list of patriarchs of the Indian Nationalist Movement. Beginning his connection with the Congress from its very outset, he continued to serve it till the evening of his life, and took it through the whole gamut of evolution, from the humble position of being a people's organ seeking redress of administrative grievances, to that of a National Assembly working for the definite object of attaining Swaraj. He singled out the young Jinnah there and then for rôles which would have done

credit to any man. Jinnah returned to India in 1896 after qualifying himself for the Bar, and was called to the Bar in 1897.

When Mahomed Ali Jinnah returned to India he was a raw youth totally inexperienced in the ways of the world. But he was soon to have his first taste of hardship and real worry. For some time things in business had been going none too well for his father and, on his return, he found him involved in heavy financial ruin. It was naturally a hard blow to the young Jinnah who, until now a favourite of fortune, was suddenly faced with unexpected poverty. Fired, however, by a generous anxiety to keep his beloved father from feeling the sting of his misfortune, he set out to conquer the world equipped with nothing but his youth, his courage and his ambition.

About the year 1897 Jinnah went to Bombay, where he expected a wider field for the exercise of his talents. The first three years were of severe hardship. But after that period his buoyant patience bore fruit. Through the kind offices of an old friend Jinnah was granted permission to read in the chambers of Mr. Macpherson, then acting Advocate-General of Bombay. It was a very courteous concession, in fact, the first of its kind to be granted to an Indian. This may be described as his start on the path to success, because with his gifts he was bound to profit very largely from this opportunity. After a short time his career became just one continuous record of successive triumphs. To-day he is considered to be a great lawyer, in fact, one of the greatest that India has produced. We may have had jurists greater than Jinnah, but surely no greater advocate. His fine advocacy became his greatest asset in the legal profession, and this, combined with his other qualities, makes him one of the greatest lawyers.

He is gifted with a unique and

characteristic style of speaking which he has carried into every sphere of life in which he has taken a part. As a speaker Mahomed Ali Jinnah has the triple assets of a magnetic presence, an impressive delivery, and a voice which while lacking in volume has an arresting timbre. His small mannerisms, gestures and the inflection of his tone, which would be at best insignificant in a smaller man, all play their part in creating that final impression which is Jinnah the public speaker. But, though occasionally he has attained a moment of wholly unconscious yet stirring eloquence, he has the cogent force of a brilliant advocate rather than the glowing fervour of a fiery orator. And it is not on a public platform, but at a round table conference that he finds full scope for his unusual powers of persuasion, luminous exposition, searching argument and impeccable judgment. Perhaps his long connection with the Bar and the legislature has had something to do with moulding the style that has become his own. His great powers as a debater have earned him the name of "parliamentary juggler." But I am anticipating. Let us go back to his entry into politics and his activities in the cause of India's freedom, which form one of the noblest chapters in his career.

Mahomed Ali Jinnah was from the outset destined to play a prominent part in politics. His rich gifts clearly marked him for such a rôle. In his political creed we find him deeply influenced by two outstanding personalities of the time. It has been mentioned elsewhere that he came into contact with Dadabhai Naoroji at a very tender and impressionable age when he first went out to England. The second figure in Indian politics which was a source of inspiration to Jinnah was Gopal Krishna Gokhale, who occupies a place of great honour and respect in the roll of India's worthy sons. He combined in himself two of the rarest gifts—a heart fired by great fervour and sincerity and an intellect of the highest order. Accordingly we

ALL-INDIA MOSLEM LEADERS' CONFERENCE

A photograph taken outside Mr. Jinnah's bungalow in Bombay where a meeting had been held.

MR. JINNAH AT LAHORE

In 1936 Mr. Jinnah visited Lahore to seek a solution to the Civil Disobedience Campaign then in force in that city. He is seen at his reception at the station about to address the crowd.

find the impress of Gokhale's personality on the movement which he nurtured with his thought and service. He was the model which Jinnah placed before himself. On one occasion, in an unguarded moment of self-revelation, Jinnah said, "It is my ambition to become the Moslem Gokhale." The true significance of these words can only be realised by those who know how secretive he is in his inner thoughts and in the revelation of his true likes and dislikes. In the light of this avowal it is interesting to recall Gokhale's own prediction about his gifted comrade. "He has true stuff in him," he said, "and that freedom from all sectarian prejudice which will make him the best ambassador of Hindu-Moslem unity." This estimate of Jinnah, generous as it sounds, is only a just tribute to his true and tried patriotism.

In 1906 Jinnah was already a rising lawyer and coming politician. We find him playing his unostentatious part in the activities of the time as Private Secretary to his old master Dadabhai Naoroji who, at the historic sessions of the National Congress at Calcutta, for the first time enunciated the glorious ideal of Self-Government for India. Jinnah had already joined the ranks of the National Congress, fired no doubt by the virile patriotism of men like Badruddin Tyabji and the lion-hearted Pherozeshah Mehta. Incidentally it is interesting to note that his maiden speech at the Congress Session was on a motion relating to Waqf Alal-aulad—a measure that was later to bring his name into such prominence. Interesting, too, and suggestive in view of succeeding events, is it to find this future leader of the Moslems present as a sort of cross-bencher at the conference of Hindu and Moslem leaders convened at Allahabad in 1910 under Sir Wamilli Wedderburn's benign direction to consider a somewhat premature and artificial *entente cordiale* between the two communities still so sharply divided by a gulf of mutual dislike and distrust.

The year 1910 has yet another importance in our present chronicle. In that year the Moslems of the Bombay Presidency elected him as their representative to the Supreme Legislative Council. At first sight it might seem incompatible for a staunch nationalist like him to represent a purely sectarian interest. But his conduct throughout convincingly proved that national and Moslem interests were not necessarily opposed to each other, and it gave the lie to the belief that anyone who tried to reconcile the two would be torn between conflicting loyalties. In the Council, Mahomed Ali Jinnah invariably lent his willing support to every liberal measure involving the larger national issues—measures like Gokhale's Elementary Education Bill and Mr. Basu's Special Marriage Bill, against which there was violent opposition from many quarters.

About this time Jinnah rendered a great service to Moslems and earned their lasting gratitude. For some time past Moslem opinion had been clamouring for a measure to counteract the effect of certain Privy Council decisions based on an interpretation of Mohammedan Law considered to be wrong and injurious. That opinion finally crystallised into the Waqf Validating Bill of 1913, to introduce which Jinnah was specially nominated for an extra term by the Viceroy, Lord Hardinge. He showed great skill and tact in piloting through such an intricate and controversial measure— the first instance of a Bill passing into law on the motion of a private member. It won him not only the wondering admiration of his colleagues but also his first meed of general recognition

from his co-religionists all over India, who, while still regarding him as a little outside the orthodox pale of Islam, were soon to seek his advice and guidance in their political affairs.

After this there was a short break in Jinnah's work as a legislator. During the three years that followed he was for a considerable time in England. His first trip was in 1913, when about the middle of April he proceeded to Europe in search of a long, idle holiday. Once in England, however, there was no rest for this tireless worker. He was drawn at once into the tangled web of the Indian Student-world, whose cause he espoused with great zeal and understanding. Within a few weeks of his arrival in London he founded the London Indian Association, which forms an excellent focus for the otherwise scattered energies and activities of young India in a foreign land. At his instance a Committee was appointed by the India Office to inquire into the legitimate grievances of Indian students suffering from restrictions which hindered their admission into educational centres.

He returned to India in the autumn of the same year, but had to go to England again in May, 1914, as member of the All-India Congress Deputation concerning the proposed reform of the India Council. On this he had already moved resolutions at the Karachi sessions of the Congress a few months earlier and at the Agra sessions of the Moslem League, with which organisation his connection had just begun and will be considered at length in due course. It was no small compliment to Jinnah that he was chosen to be the spokesman of articulate India before the representatives of the British Parliament and the British public. The leading English journals published numerous interviews, and his concise and lucid statement of the Indian

WITH THE MAHATMA

Mr. Jinnah consults with Mahatma Gandhi during discussions on Hindu-Moslem unity, an ideal dear to them both.

case which appeared in the London *Times* attracted widespread attention and comment.

In the autumn of 1916 Mahomed Ali Jinnah was once more elected by the Moslems of Bombay to the Viceregal Council. Ever since then he has almost continuously been connected with the Imperial Legislature of India, in the deliberations of which body he has taken a leading part, contributing in no small measure to raising the standard of its debates and heightening the general quality of its work. His association with the Central Legislature of India, through all its phases of evolution, has been so long and intimate that it has become difficult now to think of the one without the other. There is hardly any important enactment of the Legislature in the shaping of which he has not had a share. To-day he is considered a power in the Assembly. What is the secret of his

power? He is, of course, a powerful debater. But that is only one of the reasons for his great strength and influence. The other reason is his independence and honesty, which have all through the years characterised his work in the Assembly. As he never puts himself under the slightest obligation to the Government Benches, he can always be counted upon to have a free judgment on all matters and give expression to it without hesitation or reserve. Although he receives more than his share of requests to put in a word of recommendation here and a word there, he has steeled himself against such weakness lest it may interfere with the independence of his action on more vital issues involving much greater consequences. The purpose of his smallest move in the Assembly is to work for the good of the people, whose interests he places above everything else. It is for history to determine the relative importance of men; but, judging from Jinnah's work as a legislator alone, we find the value and volume of his services second to none. His latest contribution was the part he played in sending the Shariat Bill to the Statute Book.

One of the most unfortunate and tragic events for Moslems in Indian history was the Mutiny of 1857. The actual incidents—brutalities perpetrated on both sides—were painful enough, but the memories which it left behind were even more so. Moslems had to shoulder the major share of the blame for this unfortunate outbreak and consequently had a more bitter taste of the retribution that followed. The result was that the Moslem community as a whole became apathetic towards politics and things in general. For several decades they continued to look with suspicion upon their new rulers and similarly in their turn were held in suspicion.

After the National Congress was founded in the eighties of the nineteenth century, Moslem attitude towards it was marked by the same apathy and suspicion which characterised their entire outlook. But this unhealthy state of affairs could not last indefinitely. Gradually Moslems began to have a growing realisation that the sister community was stealing a march on them in politics just as it had already done in education. So in December, 1906, the first political meeting of Moslems was held under the presidentship of Nawab Viqarul-Mulk in which the idea of a Moslem League was mooted, and finally an organisation of that name was set up with the object of voicing current Moslem opinion and aspirations. But it was soon found to be too narrow and too nebulous in its scope and aims to keep pace with the intense and growing national consciousness. About the middle of 1912 some

important Moslem leaders met in a conference at Calcutta to reconsider a remodelling of the Constitution of the League on more progressive and patriotic lines.

Mr. Syed Wazir Hasan, who was honorary secretary of the League at the time, was sent round on an extensive tour to ascertain the views of Moslems in every province regarding so momentous a change of policy and perspective. In the following December a special meeting of the League Council was called, presided over by His Highness the Aga Khan, to consider the draft of an entirely new constitution. It was ultimately adopted with great enthusiasm at the memorable sessions of the All-India Moslem League held at Lucknow on March 22, 1913 — a date that inaugurated a new era in the political history of Moslem India.

A reference has been made earlier to the fact that Mahomed Ali Jinnah was closely associated with Congress activities from the very beginning of his public career. So, pledged to the greater national welfare, he had with characteristic independence and honesty kept himself apart from the Moslem League movement which was till then frankly and exclusively sectarian in its sympathy and purpose. He was, however, invited to attend the Calcutta Conference, and also the later Council meeting—an act of courtesy which was in itself a graceful acknowledgment of his ability and merit. He gave his informal and valuable support to Clause D of the new constitution which materially embodied the Congress ideal of:

"*Attainment under the ægis of the British Crown of a system of Self-Government suitable to India through constitutional means, by bringing about, amongst others, a steady reform of the existing system of administration by promoting national unity, by fostering*

KARACHI WELCOMES MR. JINNAH
The picturesque procession was arranged to welcome Mr. Jinnah to Karachi, where he went in 1938 to attend the Moslem League Conference.

public spirit among the people of India, and by co-operating with other communities for the said purpose."

But up till now he was not a regular member of the organisation. This came about in England, where he had gone for a holiday in 1913. In the autumn of that year on the eve of his departure for India he was approached by Maulana Mohammad Ali and Mr. Wazir Hasan to enrol himself formally as a member of the All-India Moslem League. His deep interest in the organisation, to whose expanded outlook he had contributed so signally by his example, was unquestionably there, but, before enrolment, he made it clear to his two friends that loyalty to the Moslem League and the Moslem interest would in no way and at no time imply even the shadow of disloyalty to the larger national cause to which his life was dedicated.

The years that followed are of special interest, because during this period Jinnah worked ceaselessly in the cause of complete friendship and understanding between the Hindu and Moslem communities with his characteristic sincerity and energy. His efforts were so richly rewarded that he came to be looked upon as an ambassador of Hindu-Moslem unity. To-day certain individuals and bodies cannot repeat too loudly or too often that Jinnah is a communalist and an anti-nationalist. But any fair-minded person who takes the trouble of informing himself about past history and the succession of events which drove him to his present policy cannot help being struck by the injustice of such a description.

The tragic and untimely death of Gopal Krishna Gokhale in February, 1915, brought Hindus and Moslems together in a bond of common loss and sorrow. It was increasingly felt that the time was now ripe for a more direct and definite rapprochement between the two great communities that had recently exchanged cordial expressions of good-

THE STREETS OF KARACHI DURING THE PROCESSION

will and fellowship from afar. The Indian National Congress was to hold its sittings that year in Bombay. Mahomed Ali Jinnah, supported at that time by all the leading local Moslems, sent an invitation to the All-India Moslem League to hold its next annual sessions in Bombay during the national week in December. The story of that invitation and its startling sequel is painful in its shameful and subterranean intrigue. In the hour of such grave and bitter crisis this dauntless soldier of unity rose to the heights of an invincible patriotism. With a proud and splendid indifference to all personal suffering and sacrifice, heedless alike of official dissuasion or disfavour, the aggressive malice and machinations of his opponents or even the temporary injustice of his distant friends, Mahomed Ali Jinnah strove with an incomparable devotion and courage to create that supreme moment in our national history which witnessed the birth of a new India, redeemed and victorious in the love of her united' children. An eye-witness of the grand culmination of events describes the scene in the following words: "Seldom has the pageant of time unrolled a scene so touching, so thrilling, so magnificent with drama and destiny as was enacted on the afternoon of December 30, 1915, when amidst the tears and applause of a gathered multitude the veteran heroes of the National Congress entered in a body to greet and bless their comrades of the Moslem League."

The new year dawned cloudless for this valiant fighter of national battles, bringing him some of the highest awards of his professional and public career. He added much lustre to his forensic reputation by his masterly conduct of two sensational law-suits involving respectively Mr. Horniman, the trusted friend, and Mr. Tilak the beloved tribune of the Indian people.

At this point we have to deviate a little from the thread of our narrative. About this time there was a growing surprise and reproach in the minds of his followers that so ardent an apostle of Self-Government should hold himself aloof from the recently organised Home Rule Movement which was rousing the country like a clarion call to freedom. It may have been partly due to a lingering sense of allegiance to the old school of politics in which he had been trained; or perhaps it may have been due to the habitual caution of a nature slow to commit itself to new and far-reaching responsibilities. However, the news of Mrs. Besant's internment in the June of 1917, which evoked unparalleled demonstrations throughout India, moved Mahomed Ali Jinnah to a prompt and militant decision. He immediately joined the Bombay Home Rule League. He could not remain in it as an ordinary member, but undertook, as its President, the delicate task of guiding its fortunes and guarding its interests through that troubled period of its indignant activities.

In the meantime the bonds of unity and affection in which Hindus and Moslems had been bound grew stronger and stronger. This was perhaps the most gladdening phase of a period almost heart-breaking in its disappointments. The Indian nation which had stood valiantly with its rulers in the War in the hope of winning back its freedom was soon to be rudely disillusioned. The War ended successfully for the British but, instead of bringing to Indians a realisation of their hopes, it inaugurated an era of repressive rule. Unfortunate incidents happened with astounding rapidity. The intense agitation which greeted the Rowlatt Bills and the iron hand with which the Government dealt with it will remain a sore wound in the heart of the Indian nation. Then Jilianwala Bagh: the "creeping orders" and the reign of Terror ushered in by martial law in the Punjab—and all this so soon after the War—finally destroyed any hopes which Indians might have entertained of the Government.

In this hour of their humiliation the two communities turned to each other for goodwill and affection. As a result of this understanding their policy and aims at this time were identical. The Congress espoused the cause of Khilafat, and the Moslem League fought shoulder to shoulder with the Congress in the great drive for National Freedom and Independence. In 1921 the fourteenth session of the All-India Moslem League was held in Ahmedabad with Maulana Hasrat Mohani as President. This was the seventh and last of the series held with the Congress sessions. Prominent among Congress leaders who attended the League Sessions were Messrs. Gandhi, Vijayragharacharia, Patel, Hakim Ajmal Khan and Dr. Ansari. It was a very well attended and a very successful session. Moslems were taking a complete share in the Non-Co-operation and Civil Disobedience movement started by Mahatma Gandhi and also in the suffering and sacrifice which it entailed.

A series of unfortunate incidents sounded the death-knell of the movement for the time being and of the Hindu-Moslem unity. The happenings at Chauri Chaura in the U.P., and similar incidents in Bombay and Madras compelled Mahatma Gandhi to suspend the movement which he had been unable to keep non-violent in character. All the leaders were arrested and lodged in jails. Soon after this started the series of communal riots which gradually spread to all parts of India and to this day mar the life and politics of the country.

It is not necessary for the purpose of the present narrative to try to assign or apportion blame for the riots, which will remain a disfiguring page in the history of this period. Here we are only concerned with the effect which they produced. They succeeded in shattering the Hindu-Moslem unity for which Jinnah and his band of supporters had worked so sincerely. They also succeeded in driving Jinnah out of politics, at least for the time being. The natural reaction of an inward and sensitive nature like his was deep disgust commingled with pain and sorrow. The Moslem community, in its lack of any definite policy or programme, could only be compared to a derelict vessel adrift on a stormy sea, and this condition of the community was reflected in the Moslem League.

Forces were now at work which were to turn Jinnah more and more towards the exclusive leadership of Moslems. The process, however, took the whole of the last decade to complete itself—running as it did the whole gamut from complete Hindu-Moslem unity in 1921 to an absolute break at the present day.

The announcement of the Statutory Commission in November, 1927, and the declaration of the policy and the principle underlying it stunned India by its utter lack of sympathy with Indian opinion, evoking intense and unanimous resentment. For a short time a common indignation brought together on a common platform the accredited leaders of all communities and classes, representing the most diverse interests and most divergent modes of political thought. Mahomed Ali Jinnah led the campaign of protest started in Bombay against the constitution and programme of the Statutory Commission. In his speech, delivered at the meeting of the citizens of Bombay held on December 3, Jinnah said, "I expect and I have every hope that they (Moslems) will not lag behind the Hindus in any way, but will work with you Hindus, Parsis and Christians, and go through the ordeal as a united people."

Subsequent events soon made it clear that this apparent unity and agreement was confined to the condemnation of the Simon Commission and of those who had appointed it. When it came to the formulation of a positive programme, the two principal parties were found to cling tenaciously to their respective policies and all efforts to bridge the gulf were unsuccessful. The Congress and the Hindu Mahasabha produced the Nehru Report as representing their ideas on the lines to be adopted by the proposed constitutional changes. This could not satisfy the Moslems, whose policy and demands had been taking shape for some time and were finally embodied in Jinnah's fourteen points.

The history of these points is important as it contains the clue of Jinnah's present policy and demands for the Moslems of India. The nucleus of the famous fourteen points is really the formulation of Moslem demands by Jinnah in respect of the forthcoming changes in the Indian Constitution at three successive sessions of the All-India Moslem League in the years 1924, 1925 and 1926. These related to the following:—

(1) Effective representation of minorities without reducing the majority in any province.

(2) Separate electorates.

(3) No disturbance in the Moslem majority in the Punjab, Bengal and N.W.F.P. by any territorial redistribution.

(4) Religious liberty, etc.

(5) Machinery for enforcing liberty of religion.

These proposals were criticised by the Hindu leaders, who insisted that Moslems should postulate in their scheme joint electorates with safeguards for rights and interests of Moslems. Accordingly Mahomed Ali Jinnah issued invitations to representative Mohamme-dans in all parts of India, who met at Delhi on March 20, 1927, and put forward what have come to be known as the Delhi Moslem Proposals. These accepted the principle of joint electorates if, *inter alia*, the following conditions were accepted:

(1) Sind should be separated from the Bombay Presidency and constituted into a separate province.

(2) Reforms should be introduced in the N.W.F.P. and in Baluchistan on the same footing as in any other province in India.

These proposals were substantially accepted by the All-India Congress Committee Meeting held in Bombay in May, 1927, and were later embodied in the resolution adopted at the open session of the Indian National Congress at Madras in December, 1927. The response thus made by the Congress to the Moslem proposals was considered by the session of the All-India Moslem League at Calcutta in December, 1927, and the Council of the League was authorised to appoint a sub-committee to confer with the Working Committee of the Indian National Congress for the purpose of drafting a constitution for India and of taking part in the National Convention which was going to be held in Delhi in the following March as proposed by the Congress.

The idea of drawing up an agreed constitution led to the summoning of the All Parties Conference at Delhi on February 11, 1928. This was the first and the last meeting of this conference in which the Moslem League representatives were present. The basis of rapprochement brought about by the Congress resolution at Madras and the response made by the League at Calcutta was thrown completely overboard. The All Parties Conference now struck altogether a new line, and its deliberations continued, unattended by League representatives, till at last the Nehru Report was ready for consideration.

The basic principles of the communal settlement embodied in the Nehru Report were contrary to those on which Moslem opinion had hitherto expressed its willingness to come to an agreement. The only occasion on which the League gave its consideration to the Nehru Report was when it was invited to send a delegation to the All Parties Convention at Calcutta in December, 1928. The proposals submitted by the League delegates were summarily rejected by the Convention. Thus ended the efforts to bring about a settlement between the Hindu and Moslem communities.

What took place at the two Round Table Conferences in London is comparatively recent history. Mahomed Ali Jinnah and other Moslem leaders took their stand on the demands contained in the Fourteen Points. Hindu leaders, and specially those of the Hindu Mahasabha, declared that the Nehru Report had already gone too far and there was no room for the slightest further concession. The one man who could have brought about a settlement was Mahatma Gandhi. But he contented himself with signing a blank cheque for the Moslems, leaving it to themselves to cash it if they could from the Hindus. The interminable quarrels and recriminations which were a feature of the whole business were brought to an end by the announcement of the Communal Award.

The Hindu-Moslem problem to-day remains as unsolved and insoluble as ever. Hindu-Moslem unity, for which Jinnah had striven so vigorously, became a fact in 1920. But once again Time has changed that victory into defeat. False hopes of a settlement were raised a number of times, but it is still very much out of sight. There was a lengthy correspondence between Jinnah and

Gandhi on the one hand, and Jinnah and Nehru on the other. There were talks also between the same gentlemen with the same result. Pandit Jawaharlal Nehru's letters, which may be taken to represent fairly the Congress attitude towards this matter, dismiss the points raised by Jinnah as too trivial to bother about at a time when the country and the world are faced with problems of much greater moment. It has, however, not occurred to Pandit Nehru and others of the Congress that the triviality of these demands is just one more reason they should be done with and the way cleared for meeting the greater issues.

At present Mahomed Ali Jinnah is about sixty-three years of age, and in spite of his delicate health his great devotion to the cause which he is serving enables him to do an amount of work which would be the wonder and despair of a much younger man. It will be an apt ending to this short account of the life and achievements of this remarkable man to give a pen portrait of him by Mrs. Sarojini Naidu: "Never was there a nature whose outer qualities provided so complete an antithesis of its inner worth. Tall and stately, but thin to the point of emaciation, languid and luxurious of habit, Mahomed Ali Jinnah's attenuated form is the deceptive sheath of a spirit of exceptional vitality and endurance. Somewhat formal and fastidious, and a little aloof and imperious of manner, the calm hauteur of his accustomed reserve but masks for those who know him a naïve and eager humanity, an intuition quick and tender as a woman's, a humour gay and winning as a child's. Pre-eminently rational and practical, discreet and dispassionate in his estimate and acceptance of life, the obvious sanity and serenity of his worldly wisdom effectually disguise a shy and splendid idealism which is of the very essence of the man."

THE RT. HON. SIR AKBAR HYDARI, NAWAB HYDER NAWAZ JUNG
BAHADUR, P.C.

Prime Minister of Hyderabad.

The Rt. Hon. SIR AKBAR HYDARI, P.C.

A MAKER OF MODERN HYDERABAD
BORN 1869

BY ROBERT BRYAN

THE state of Hyderabad stretches over an area nearly equal to that of Italy, on the high Deccan plateau that separates the Arabian Sea from the Bay of Bengal. Its size alone gives it and, ever since Asaf Jah, the Mogul emperor's viceroy in the Deccan, defeated the forces of Delhi in 1724 and asserted his independence, has given it, great importance in the history of India; moreover, it is the only great Moslem state south of the River Narbada. There were periods, however, throughout the nineteenth century when the state, laxly administered, declined in power and prestige. But with the coming of more modern ideas it has achieved that measure of re-organisation and enlightened progress which has enabled it to take its rightful place in the New India that is so rapidly taking shape. Among the makers of modern Hyderabad, Sir Akbar Hydari will always take an honoured place.

Mohamed Akbar Nyzarali Hydari was born in Bombay, of prosperous merchant stock, on November 8, 1869. His father, in pursuit of business interests, had made six voyages to China; on his mother's side were relatives who had travelled to England and elsewhere. From the first he knew an enlightened home in which narrowness of mind was conspicuous by its absence. His family was of the Jamaat Sulaimani (Bohra) sect of Moslems; the shaping of his views in later life may have been influenced by the fact that he was descended neither from the Moslem conquerors of the thirteenth century onwards nor from converted Hindus. The Bohras,

moving eastwards for trading purposes in the ninth and tenth centuries, had settled on the Konkan coast as merchants —not warrior-conquerors. Though devout Moslems, their descendants do not inherit militant fanaticism; and in Akbar Hydari this characteristic, to be seen in so many Indian Moslems, has never been present.

Akbar Hydari was educated at the Jesuit College of St. Xavier in Bombay, where he took his degree at the age of seventeen. He had studied widely: English literature, economics, Latin, history, and above all the Law. With the example of his uncle, Badruddin Tyabji, who had won fame as a judge, before him, he planned for himself a legal career; he was prominent in debate at countless club and society debates. His family, however, thought otherwise; a career in the financial service was, they told him, to be his fate. He has told how he considered that he "hadn't a ghost of a chance" as he sat for the examination, for the subject, he thought at the time, was alien to him; but his name was first on the list of successful candidates, so, again to quote his own words, "I entered the Finance Department with tears."

That was in 1888, and by 1903 he had risen, by way of a variety of posts, to be Controller of Central Treasuries. Assistant Accountant General in the United Provinces in 1890, Deputy Accountant General at Madras (the first Indian ever to hold the post) in 1900, Examiner of the Government of India Press Accounts in 1901, these were some of the posts he held before entering the service of Hyderabad State in 1905. It is true that by the closing years of the last century Indians were being admitted in increasing numbers into the government service, but it was still the exception rather than the rule that they should achieve positions of great responsibility; in the circumstances then prevailing, Akbar Hydari's rise in these early years of his career was spectacular. He proved himself a sound as well as far-sighted administrator, notable for the lucidity with which he expressed his views and arguments.

The achievements with which his name is, to date, chiefly associated occurred later when he was finance and railway member of the Hyderabad State Executive Council; but his time in British India helped him to formulate those principles upon which his subsequent actions have been based. Particularly as Examiner of Government Press Accounts he travelled widely throughout India, coming into contact with all aspects of the vast Indian community. Slowly but surely his conception of a land where Hindu and Moslem should appreciate each other's good qualities took shape. Long afterwards he was magnificently to express this conception in a presidential speech to the All-India Mohammedan Educational Conference at Calcutta:

"It will not be the growth but the death of Indian Nationalism if the Moslems of India fail to be impressed by the greatness of Asoka, Chandragupta, or filled with pride and joy at the immortal frescoes of Ajanta and the sculptured monuments of Ellora, or fail to derive fresh inspiration from the glorious songs of Jayadev and Tukaram, or find food for deep and satisfying thought in the discourse of Sri Krishna and Gautama the Buddha. It will not be the growth but the death of Indian Nationalism if the Hindus are not filled with pride at the architectural splendours of the Moguls and the Adil Shahis, at the political achievements of great rulers like Sher Shah and Akbar, at the fine heroism of noble queens like Chand Bibi and Nur Jehan, at the liberal statesmanship of devoted ministers like Mahmud Gavan and Abul Fazl, at the wide learning of scholars like Al Beruni and Faizi or at the inspiration of poets like Amir Khusru and Ghalib. It will be a sad day indeed if the minds of Hindu and Moslem alike are not stirred with the high and noble aims of the Viceroys like Mayo and Ripon, of administrators like Munro and Elphinstone, of friends of India like Fawcett and Bright, of missionaries like Hare and Miller. For all these and many more, whether Hindu, Moslem or Christian, loved India and worked for her."

He was a man of great authority and prestige when he spoke those words, but even when a young and comparatively unknown servant of the Government of India he had voiced the same sentiments. The concluding paragraph of an article which he contributed in 1901 to a volume on Indian Social Reform reads as follows:

"I can conceive no nobler work to which an Indian can consecrate himself than that of cementing the hearts of the diverse races and nationalities of our vast continent into a solid and united whole, bound by a union that is not merely a superficial one or that merely enables the Hindu and the Moslem, the Parsi and the Christian, to regard each other on sufferance or even with a species of benevolent neutrality, but a living and active union whereby they come to look upon each other as brothers working for the cultivation and progress of their common heritage."

From 1905 to 1920 Akbar Hydari served the state of Hyderabad, first as

Accountant General, then from 1907 as Financial Secretary and finally from 1911 as Secretary to the Home Department. His financial acumen bore fruit in the reorganisation of the state finances so that each state department was given a separate triennial contract. Under the previous centralised system enterprise was stifled, for no department ever knew how much in any given year would be allotted to them to spend; Akbar Hydari opened up by this measure new channels through which the great wealth of the state could flow. Tolerant to additional expenditure where it was likely to have a constructive effect, he insisted also on the building up of reserves to deal with such matters as famine and flood. Famine when it visits the Deccan is perhaps more terrible than anywhere else in India. Less frequent than in more barren parts of the peninsula, it strikes more terribly, for in the Deccan there

are more mouths to feed. Akbar Hydari's famine reserve fund has done much to mitigate its horrors.

Akbar Hydari had married in 1893 Amena Tyabji. It was with her aid that he fought against the rigours of the Purdah system. If there can be no doubt of his devotion to the Moslem creed, there can be as little of his liberal interpretation thereof. His wife, at his encouragement and with his support, was the first Moslem woman to appear in public in Bombay out of purdah, and in Hyderabad she set the same example. Presiding at the first Hyderabad Educational Conference in 1915, Akbar Hydari said: "That country can never be educated or progressive whose women are steeped in ignorance. . . . If the mothers who give our children their first lessons in life—lessons which must inevitably influence their entire future— are devoid of education, how can we be

MEETING OF THE LEGISLATIVE COUNCIL

Sir Akbar Hydari, presiding, announced the command of H.E.H. the Nizam for the formation of a Reform Committee.

ROYAL WEDDING

Sir Akbar Hydari (extreme left) at the marriage of the Nizam of Hyderabad's second son, Prince Muazzam Jah Bahadur.

sure that when the children go out of their hands they will be blessed with real education and morals?" To many to-day this statement may seem so obvious as to be a truism, but it must be remembered that Akbar Hydari is a Moslem and a servant of the premier Moslem state in India, and that what he was maintaining ran contrary to the orthodox Moslem tradition of many centuries.

Akbar Hydari made his reputation in Hyderabad as a financial expert; he increased it in other ways in the years after 1911 when he was in charge of the Home Department. To him the state owes the setting up of its archæological department. Within the borders of the state lie the caves of Ajanta and Ellora, the ruins of the great fortress of Daulatabad, the remains of the architectural glories of Bidar and Gulbarga, and many other relics of the Bahmani and later dynasties. Too long had these been neglected; their care, and researches into their origins, became, under Akbar Hydari's influence, a chief concern of the state.

It was in these years that he conceived the idea of a state university, the main concern of which would be to teach through the vernacular and by so doing to confer upon Indian students for the first time the supreme advantage of acquiring Western learning through the medium of a familiar idiom. The Osmania University at Hyderabad—the result of this idea—is certainly one of his chief claims to fame. Urdu is the language in which all general subjects are taught, and a bureau has been set up for the translation of Western text-books and of Western scientific and literary researches into this language. The Osmania was the first university in India conceived upon this principle. Its success has been considerable; the students benefit enormously from pur-suing their studies in a familiar medium; and among its repercussions has been an advance in elementary education throughout the state. There is one, perhaps unavoidable, handicap. India has no single language; and Urdu, although intelligible to millions in the north, is not the "vernacular" of the majority of the population of Hyderabad. Specifically the university is not in-tended primarily for Moslems; the aim is that all communities in the state should benefit equally from it. Nevertheless, local students who are Moslems must start with a big initial advantage. The problem of language, if any attempt is made to get away from a sectarian basis in education, is common to all India,

and it cannot be said that the Osmania University has solved it; at least, however, it has proved that there are tangible advantages to students in conveying higher education in a mother tongue.

In 1920 Akbar Hydari reverted for a brief period to service in British India as Accountant General in Bombay, but in the following year he returned to service in Hyderabad as Finance and Railway Member of the State Executive Council, a post he held until 1937 when he was appointed President of that body. In the ten years after 1921 the financial policy which he had earlier instituted bore fruit. The state treasury proved itself capable of shouldering the burden of large irrigation, famine relief and other schemes so successfully that the state was able without difficulty to float loans in the Indian market at $3\frac{1}{2}$ per cent.; and in 1930 it took over from private owner-ship 1,200 miles of railway, paying out of income a sum equivalent to more than eight million pounds sterling. As Finance

HIGH COURT, HYDERABAD

One of the fine modern buildings erected in the city of Hyderabad is the High Court, lying to the west of the Afzalganj Gate.

Member, Akbar Hydari enhanced the reputation that he had won as a subordinate. He was knighted in 1928.

In the realm of education his interests had for long ranged beyond the borders of the state he served. If the Osmania University was his favourite child, he was keenly interested also in the Universities of Dacca, Calcutta, Bombay and Aligarh. He was president of the All-India Mohammedan Educational Conference in 1917, and he played a prominent part in 1921 in countering the attempts of the brothers Ali to win over the Aligarh University to Non-Co-operation. He was by 1925, as far as education was concerned, an all-India figure, incurring praise as well as condemnation from extreme congressmen and also, through his broad-minded views, from the extreme section of orthodox Moslems. He was made at various times a fellow of Bombay, Dacca and Aligarh Universities, as well as of the Osmania. As a political figure and statesman he first emerged into real prominence on the all-India stage in the course of the events that culminated in the first Round Table Conference in London in 1930-32. From that period his rôle has been a leading one.

The discussions and events that from 1930-37 led up to the formulation of a scheme of federal government for India and the putting into effect of Provincial Autonomy, formed a large part of the background to his career. He headed the Hyderabad Delegation to the Round Table Conference, and was the state's representative on the Select Committee on Indian Constitutional Reform appointed by the British Parliament in 1933. In 1934 he was Chairman of the Committee of Indian State Ministers.

Even when Hyderabad had been feeble of purpose and ill-governed, as it was for part of the nineteenth century, it was a force with which the British

Government had always seriously to reckon. The support of the same state, well and efficiently governed, may be said to have been essential to the success of any federal scheme. From the first, Sir Akbar Hydari made it clear at numerous meetings in London of the Round Table Conference that he considered some sort of federation in which representatives of the states should sit in the Central Government with representatives from the provinces was essential to India's future, and he made it equally clear that he saw the necessity, and was prepared for, a surrender of some of the powers which, within their own borders, the various states exercised.

He was not alone in these views. The representatives of Mysore and Gwalior —to name two states—shared them, but his influence was immense and probably decisive in persuading the whole body of states to accept the federal idea. His point of view is put clearly in an article written by him early in 1937:

"The idealism which inspired the States at the early stages of the discussions to accept the idea of an organic association of an all-India legislature had not died down. The ideal of a self-governing India . . . could not be achieved for British India alone, and the States' readiness to throw into the common scales some of their own powers and authorities in order to assist that realisation, testifies to the inherent greatness of their traditions which permitted, despite a long history of unconcern with the rest of India, the vision of all-India to be conceived."

The end of this passage is as significant as its beginning. What he advocated in these years was a complete break in the policy pursued by the Indian States at least since the Indian Mutiny. As he himself stated: "The acceptance by the majority of States of the idea of

THE OLD CITY—

Flower stalls in the old bazaar, Hyderabad. These and much of the buildings in the vicinity are condemned under the City Town Improvement Scheme. They will come down to make room for modern well-planned and built houses.

—AND THE NEW

Playing fields and new houses built under the Town Improvement Scheme in Hyderabad. The improvement of housing conditions for the people of Hyderabad is one of the schemes to which Sir Akbar has given close, personal attention.

THE OSMANIA HOSPITAL, HYDERABAD

federation . . . is almost revolutionary." He believed, when he went to the Round Table Conference, that such acceptance was right, that the previous attitude of the states had "led to the growth of an artificial unconcern with developments outside their territories," but from the start he was on his guard lest what the states gained might be more than counter-balanced by what they were asked to give up. He was throughout the representative of the chief Indian State who, out of loyalty to his ruler but also because he believed that Hyderabad and other states had much to give to a united India, was determined that their sovereignty should be reserved to them. He was prepared, eager for federation, but for federation on terms which would ensure the states' survival. Nor can he be blamed, in view of the speeches and actions of leading members of the Congress party, for insisting that

adequate precautions be taken to make their survival reasonably certain.

It was on Sir Akbar Hydari's initiative that the problem of Berar, which had for long complicated relations between Hyderabad and the Government of India, was settled. This territory, lying to the north of the Nizam's dominions, had been ceded to the British in 1853, this arrangement having been modified —but in a typically high-handed way— by Lord Curzon in 1902, when it was leased in perpetuity by the Nizam to the Government of India. In 1926 a reconsideration of the whole question was requested, which the Viceroy, Lord Reading, refused on the ground that "No ruler of an Indian State can justifiably claim to negotiate with the British Government on an equal footing." Yet ten years later Sir Akbar Hydari achieved exactly that basis of negotiation. It is improbable that he obtained all that he desired; the administration of Berar is still carried on by the Government of the Central Provinces, but the right to be consulted on various specified matters has been reserved to the Nizam, his sovereignty over the territory has been recognised, and the perpetual lease has been abolished. What had in 1926 been denied entirely to Hyderabad was in 1936 to a considerable extent granted. By able diplomacy, well supported by his great reputation as a statesman of balanced integrity, Sir Akbar Hydari achieved that basis of negotiation on terms of equality which ten years earlier had been unthinkable.

Sir Akbar Hydari's claim to greatness, to a secure place in Indian history, must be based mainly upon two characteristics: upon his broad-mindedness and upon his ability to look ahead. The former is shown most notably in his attitude to what in India are almost twin subjects, religion and education. Though a profound believer in Islam, he could yet realise that others might be entirely justified in believing equally profoundly the precepts of the great Hindu or Parsi teachers, the teachings of Christ or Gautama; and such realisation is extremely rare in profound believers of any description. Where religious tradition, as in the case of purdah, seemed to him anti-progressive, he discouraged it; where it tended to provoke civil discord, he endeavoured always to suppress it. The value of such an attitude in a Moslem state with a preponderantly Hindu population is not lightly to be underestimated.

And in educational matters he acted and advised always on the same principles. The Osmania University has, it is true, been criticised; but criticism cannot obscure the intention behind its inception. Of that intention there can be no doubt. In Akbar Hydari's own words: "Do not, I pray you, regard movements of this kind (Osmania University) as in any way separatist, or provincial or sectarian. They are based upon the first principles of self-respect, reverence, and respect for your cultural traditions which are

THE TOWN HALL, HYDERABAD

not the insidious enemies but the strongest supporters of a National Evolution." In all his dealings with, and advice to, educational bodies outside as well as inside Hyderabad State he made clear his conception of the main function of education in India: to fuse the various creeds, castes and social units of the Peninsula into a community, mutually forbearing, mutually helpful.

It is in the political sphere that his ability to look ahead is most noticeable. It must be remembered that in 1930, when he attended the first Round Table Conference, he had been, with one small interval, a servant for 25 years of the premier Indian state, and that he had been largely instrumental in raising that state to a position of power, prosperity and great prestige. This did not prevent him from realising that in the interests of a future united India the position of Hyderabad and of all the other Indian States must be modified; and in a united India he profoundly believed. Subject only to the operation of paramountcy—to the right consistently upheld but where a state was well-governed, sparingly if sometimes arbitrarily exercised—of the Government of India to interfere where necessary with their affairs—the states had for long enjoyed immunity from the turbulent problems that were always arising in British India. Sir Akbar Hydari realised that it was their duty to take a part in those problems and to surrender some of their privileges in order to do so. Only thus could India as a whole prove to the British its ability to govern itself.

It has been said that in later years his conviction of the practicability of federation wavered, that he was prepared for, if not reconciled to, the abandonment of the whole scheme. For the latter assertion there is little justification, and for his caution the attitude of

THE DURBAR HALL. PUBLIC GARDENS, HYDERABAD

the more extreme elements—both communal and political—in British India afforded considerable excuse. A mixture of realist and idealist, he saw no reason why Congress should take all and give nothing. In his conception of a united India there was room for the democratic lion to lie down with the lamb of modified autocracy. He could hardly with a clear conscience have continued to serve a state had he felt otherwise. Moreover he was convinced that any violent change from one system to the other must lead to a state of chaos out of which no good would come. He insisted, therefore, on safeguards which would insure the future integrity of the states with as much insistence as his opponents demanded that such safeguards should be non-existent. His conception of the India of the future differs in fact widely from that held by Pandit Jawaharlal Nehru or Subhas Chandra Bose. The latter envisage an India independent, radically changed, freed from the British connection. Akbar Hydari conceives of an India

equally independent but a partner in the British Commonwealth of Nations —an India in which the old and new shall be blended, the best traditions of the former and the more fruitful ideas of the latter being preserved. But in spite of all their differences he and Pandit Nehru do agree on one fundamental—on the need for an India that is in truth united.

Sir Akbar Hydari has been honoured by his ruler, and he was made a Privy Councillor in 1936; his judgments are respected, even by those whose point of view is radically different from his own, throughout the length and breadth of India. Tolerant, ever ready to listen, capable both of giving and receiving friendship, subtle in diplomacy but with a subtlety that is based on conviction and not on pliability, he has sought not only the good of his state but of India as a whole. For this alone, and because on many occasions his influence has been decisive for progress, he would deserve to rank among the great Indians of history

SIR TEJ BAHADUR SAPRU

SIR TEJ BAHADUR SAPRU

GREATEST AUTHORITY ON INDIAN CONSTITUTIONAL LAW

BORN 1875

BY C. F. ANDREWS

MY first meeting with Tej Bahadur Sapru was in Allahabad nearly thirty-four years ago, when I went there late in the cold weather of 1906. He was then just 31 years old, for he was born on December 6th, 1875. My own work at that time was in Delhi at St. Stephen's College, near to the Kashmir Gate, and I had heard much about the intellectual brilliance of the younger school of political thinkers in the centre of the United Provinces.

Just before paying this visit to Allahabad I had received some rather painful public attention owing to a series of letters which I had written to the daily papers, protesting against a very bitter attack made on the educated classes as "seditious" and "disloyal" people. Therefore, when I visited Allahabad soon after, the leading barristers, who were members of the Congress, cordially invited me to join them at an evening function where we could talk freely concerning the strained relations between the two races. I looked forward to this meeting with eagerness, and was not disappointed. At Delhi I had found a lamentable backwardness in all political matters. This lack of interest, combined with a somewhat indolent attitude, appeared to me to be entirely undemocratic. The educated classes were suppressing their real opinions and allowing things they disliked to continue by a mere passive acceptance of them.

All this had troubled me considerably since I had come out to India. So when this evening function took place at Allahabad, with Tej Bahadur Sapru in the chair, my mind was full of the subject, and I spoke strongly about the evil which must necessarily result where ever mutual frankness was impossible between two different races.

Some of the older among those present defended the order of things that then prevailed. "We cannot help ourselves," they said to me. "We are obliged to say one thing to people like you, and another thing to the officials."

"Do you always act in this manner?" I asked with a shock of surprise.

"We cannot help it," was the answer, "for we are a subject people." Words like these made me feel almost desperate and I spoke out my mind quite freely.

The incident, small as it is, has remained vividly with me ever since; and I can picture the scene even to-day. The only one who stood by me and shared my strong indignation was the chairman, Tej Bahadur Sapru. He acknowledged at once the deep-seated wrong of it all, and offered no defence. He condemned it with a sincerity of shame that revealed his own character. While doing so, he used one argument that went right home to me and evidently touched many of those present who were far more orthodox than he was. He declared that as long as they were content to remain in social and domestic bondage they weakened their claim for political freedom. That truly valid argument has been used not only in India, but in every country that seeks to obtain Swaraj. Mahatma Gandhi has employed it with great effect in order to bring about the removal of untouchability.

When the meeting was over, Sapru

came up to me and shook my hand very warmly and thanked me most cordially for what I had said. He had evidently been deeply moved. After that we talked together long into the night, and I felt that we had become friends.

He was by far the clearest thinker whom I had ever met so far in India, and my mind went along with his all the way as I recognised his rugged honesty of purpose. It was also quite easy to see that he was a strong conservative by nature in spite of the radical background of his idea.

The greatest contrast to him, in almost every direction, was Pandit Madan Mohan Malaviya, the champion of Hindu orthodoxy. He was far more intimately associated with the Congress than Sapru was; he was also intensely religious, while Sapru was sceptically minded in all religious matters. Malaviya used to model his long English speeches on Gladstone, who was his master. They were full of oratorical appeals, and on that account were regarded in India as a triumph of English eloquence. They did not move me personally because I had got past the age when such a style was impressive. People, however, who could hardly understand his English used to listen with rapt attention just as they would listen to Surendrenath Banerjea in Bengal. They were moved, not so much by what he said as by the flow of words which came pouring out of his mouth.

Sapru's English speeches were of an entirely different character. They were always terse and closely to the point, without any superfluous words. He brought into them the forensic style with which he would plead a case in court. He was a debater rather than an orator, and did not even care to sway the multitudes by emotional appeals. Though radical in outlook, he was always somewhat of an aristocrat and too intellectual to be popular. In many ways his keenly critical mind was a hindrance to him in politics and prevented him from ever successfully leading a party.

It is interesting to me to review the present from the background of those days, and to note how far these two leaders in Allahabad, Malaviya and Sapru, who are so different in character, have drifted apart both in thought and action. We can see this not only in the political field, but even more with regard to social customs. Yet on one side they have become united, for each of them remained a constitutionalist at heart, even during the period of Non-Co-operation which followed the World War. Sapru left the National Congress as soon as ever the Non-Co-operation movement began. Even before that he had never had any sympathy with the earlier extremist position during the years 1907-1916, when the Congress was divided; and he refused to non-co-operate in 1920.

Malaviya, on the other hand, who also had never sided with the extremists in earlier days, continued to hang on as a member of the Congress, often in a minority of one, long after Non-Co-operation had been accepted as a national programme. Yet with regard to social custom his orthodoxy had remained almost entirely unshaken. The only point where it immediately gave way, at the trumpet call of Mahatma Gandhi, was with regard to "Temple Entry." Here, with a bravery that few of us were able to realise at the time, he had changed his whole manner of life and become the most ardent champion for the removal of untouchability.

Sapru, as I have already shown, had all along been a rebel at heart in these social and caste matters. He had spoken out in quite unorthodox fashion against many anti-social practices, such as child marriage, etc. Indeed, he had remained a rebel as a Hindu right up to the end. But, to-day, caste itself has moved so far forward that his earlier rebel actions would now be considered (at least in the North of India) to be quite normal and common-place.

Perhaps here is the best place to describe something of his character as I have known him. First, as I have already noted, there is a rugged independence, combined with a strong and rooted dislike for anything violent or unconstitutional. Quite regardless of consequences in speaking out the truth, even where he has to suffer for doing so, he is by his exact legal training almost over-conservative in action. Secondly, along with a very warm heart towards his own intimate circle of friends, he has deep down in his nature a close family love for all those who are nearly related to him, which makes his home in Allahabad a delightful place to stay in. Then again, he is a much travelled man, to whom Europe is almost as familiar as India. While intensely a lover of his own country and of the Urdu language (in which he writes as a master) he has become also a citizen of the world. One of his greatest relaxations is to take part in some literary contest in Urdu.

To return to the incident at Allahabad in 1906, I went on direct from there to Calcutta, in order to attend the session of the National Congress, over which Dadabhai Naoroji was presiding. There I saw for the first time Bepin Chandra Pal, Aurobindo Ghose, and others who were the new leaders in Bengal. That was my earliest education in Bengali politics, and it came almost as a shock to me after my experience in Delhi. For I had been living—so I now found out—in a "backward tract" in Delhi, where the old submissive temperament was still somnolently passive and inert.

Allahabad had been a "half-way house;" but here, in Bengal, revolt was in the very air. The English style of dress the polished English speech (which still prevailed at Allahabad) had all been thrown aside. The Bengali dress and language were everywhere dominating. Whenever men spoke to me in English it was to tell me about the injustice of the Partition. Lord Curzon had accelerated this transformation by his imperious challenges. Poets, like Rabindranath Tagore, had composed songs of revolution, and all Bengal was singing them. A full Swadeshi movement was carrying the whole country by storm. There was a world of difference between the Bengali oratory of Bepin Chandra Pal as he addressed a huge crowd in Calcutta, and the clear-cut, incisive English speech, fastidiously accurate, of Tej Bahadur Sapru, in a select gathering at Allahabad.

After the Congress was over I met Sapru again and talked about the future with him. About that time, or a little later, I began to form one clear opinion of him, namely, that his mind was wedded to Law and not to Politics. The latter would only interest him as far as it brought up problems of the Indian Constitution. For he was not by temperament a general practitioner at the Bar, though he took up civil and criminal cases as a matter of practice and was a keen lawyer. But his heart had always been in constitutional law; and on this subject he could speak with an authority greater than that of any contemporary lawyer in India.

I must hurry on to refer to his work on the Imperial Legislative Council during the latter part of the War. No one probably rendered more active help to the Government of India as an adviser at that critical juncture: for Sapru was as blunt of speech as he was independent of character.

Let me give one small incident at this point from my own experience, for it illustrates Sapru's kindness and also his independence. There had been an evil system called "Indentured Indian Labour" whereby the British Colonies had been allowed to recruit labourers from the United Provinces, Bihar and Madras. The Government of India had become convinced at last of the evils of such recruiting and had agreed to abolish the whole indenture system. But later on they had weakly accepted a compromise and agreed to continue it for another five years in order to suit the planters. I had been to Fiji and Natal and had told Sapru about the evils I had seen and heard, and he was as indignant about them as I was.

We held a public meeting in Allahabad. Mr. H. S. L. Polak was to speak about South Africa, and I was to speak about Fiji. Both of us were staying with Sapru, who was helping the cause in every way possible. Then, suddenly, I was taken ill with a cholera-attack of a very virulent kind which seemed at one time to be nearly fatal. Never can I forget the kindness of my host on that occasion and the incessant care that was taken of me by the doctor whom he called in to treat me. It was impossible for me to attend the meeting, but Sarojini Naidu read a message from me and Sapru himself spoke strongly condemning the Government compromise. Polak also told the vast audience about the evils of indenture in Natal. That important public protest in Allahabad, along with others of the same character, helped to sound the death knell of the whole indenture system.

During those days which I spent in Sapru's house my friendship with him was cemented by the long illness from which I suffered. That special occasion afterwards played a prominent part in his own life, because it gave him a new

interest in Indians abroad and made him the true champion of their cause at the Imperial Conference in 1923. He will always be remembered in India on account of his indignant challenge to General Smuts, who had refused to allow any citizenship to Indians domiciled in South Africa.

"We claim, along with you," said Sapru, "equal citizenship in the same Empire. We are *not* willing to be relegated from King George's dining-hall to King George's stables."

Rarely has the case for equal citizenship been put more forcibly than that. This one remark about King George's stables left a deep impression. On this racial question no one has spoken out with more burning indignation than Sapru, and he has nobly maintained the *izzat* of India on this and other occasions.

At the end of the same year, 1923, Sapru presided over the All-India Liberal Conference at Poona. He expressed there, also, his wrathful indignation at the inferior racial treatment of Indians abroad. While he had been unable, as we have seen, to identify himself any longer with the Congress, he had remained absolutely at one with Mahatma Gandhi with regard to this scandalous treatment of Indians abroad. On such a subject all parties in India are combined, and all take the same attitude. The Government of India has sided with them, and the Indian States also. Hindus, Moslems, Parsis and Christians alike are of one mind in rejecting the inferior status imposed on Indians in Kenya and South Africa.

Another opportunity of seeing a good deal of Sir Tej Bahadur Sapru was in Lord Reading's time, when he was Law Member. He followed Sir Sankara Nair, who had resigned after the Punjab disturbances. No more difficult post could have been offered anyone at such a critical time and it required resolution on his part to accept it. I know from personal experience how greatly the Viceroy relied on his counsel, and how frank Dr. Sapru was in offering unpalatable advice.

Whenever I went to Simla during those difficult years I used to stay with the Law Member. On one occasion he put to me a pointed question, which had evidently come from the highest authority, in order to elicit my opinion. It ran as follows: "How would you meet this new movement called Non-Co-operation?"

I replied at once, almost without thinking, "Co-operate in social uplift work, such as Prohibition, and on all questions with regard to Indians abroad."

Looking back, as I can now do, it seems to me that this advice was practical. As long as a sense of good humour remained, and also a sense of decency and humanity, the movement could be conducted on both sides in a gentlemanly manner, even though suffering was inevitable. But in the later stages, when good humour was lost, the conditions of the struggle went rapidly from bad to worse.

Though Dr. Sapru retained a profound respect for Mahatma Gandhi's character, it was easy for me to see that he could not appreciate his ideas. These remained almost a sealed book to him, and any profession of civil disobedience definitely annoyed him as a constitutional lawyer. I was constantly absent in South Africa from 1924 to 1927. Dr. Sapru had already retired from the Viceroy's Council, and as I was abroad I saw very little of him for some years. He remained in India and accomplished some very valuable work on what was called the Reforms Committee. On different occasions, also, at a later date he did his utmost to act as "peacemaker," when there seemed some possibility of a

successful intervention between the Congress leaders and the Government, which might satisfactorily conclude the Non-Co-operation struggle. Being a Liberal and a Moderate, the whole movement of which Mahatma Gandhi was the leader distressed him beyond measure and he was never reconciled to the mode of direct action which had been adopted.

Perhaps the saddest years in Sir Tej Bahadur Sapru's own political life were those which he spent in London during the almost interminable Committees and Conferences concerning the New Constitution from 1929 to 1934. He gave the best part of his time to this work and in the end was profoundly disappointed with the results. Not one of the main issues for which he had fought so strenuously was granted. In the end, the new Constitution, passed through Parliament, was an imposed Constitution and not one decided by conference and discussion. Strangely enough, it is not realised, in the midst of world confusion, how quickly the sands are running out, and also how impossible it is to answer with a clear conscience the new imperial claims from Germany and Italy, without drastically revising our own British policy towards India. For if India were really free and independent to-day, as South Africa and Canada are, it would be much easier to reply to Hitler and Mussolini with the world's moral approval.

In recent years, Sir Tej Bahadur Sapru has retired from public life. He has gone back to his own profession as a lawyer, which occupies most of his time and attention. His son has taken a leading part in the Council of State and has recently returned from Australia, where he attended the Sydney Celebrations. His political views are similar to those of his father and he takes after him in character. May both live long enough to see the fruits of all their labour!